Federal Tax Treatment

of

Foreign Income

Studies of Government Finance

TITLES PUBLISHED

* Published by the Princeton University Press. All other titles published by the Brookings Institution.

Federal Tax Treatment

of Foreign Income

LAWRENCE B. KRAUSE AND KENNETH W. DAM

A background paper prepared for a conference of experts held April 23-24, 1964, together with a summary of the conference discussion

Studies of Government Finance

THE BROOKINGS INSTITUTION

WASHINGTON, D.C.

Foreword

In 1961, THE TREASURY DEPARTMENT PROPOSED that the income from American subsidiaries operating abroad be taxed when earned. The proposal aroused a substantial controversy, which raged over the tax principles of equity and neutrality and over the consequences of foreign investment for the balance of payments of the United States. The present widespread concern over the U. S. balance of payments makes a careful study of the tax treatment of foreign income necessary. To clarify the issues involved in the taxation of foreign-source income, a conference was held at the Brookings Institution on April 23 and 24, 1964. The purpose of the conference was to provide an opportunity for a group of experts to review the major controversial issues, analyze the provisions of the present law, and clarify the differences of opinion with regard to this aspect of the tax system. This volume is comprised of both a summary of that conference and a background study prepared for it.

The volume represents the joint efforts of many people. Kenneth W. Dam of the Law School at the University of Chicago prepared most of the material appearing in Chapters II and III. His material was substantially supplemented by a paper prepared by Peggy Musgrave of the University of Pennsylvania on the new provisions enacted in the Revenue Act of 1962. Lawrence B. Krause of the senior staff of the Brookings Institution summarized the conference and is primarily responsible for Chapters I and IV. Emanuel Demos of Harvard University assisted him. Appendix A was also prepared by Kenneth W. Dam. Leslie Mills and Henry J. Gumpel of Price Waterhouse & Company prepared Appendix B. Helpful assistance was provided by Evelyn Breck, Virginia Parker, and Stephen Salant. Helen B. Eisenhart prepared the index.

The conference was attended by thirty-three experts, including attorneys, accountants, and economists from universities, research institutions, government agencies, and private practices, representing various opinions. The participants were invited in their personal capacities and not as representatives of the organizations with which they are affiliated.

While the authors assume full responsibility for this book, they wish to acknowledge the generous help they received from many people in preparation of the manuscript. In particular, they wish to thank Roy Blough, Walter Blum, Joseph A. Pechman, and Dan Throop Smith.

This volume is another Brookings publication in the series of Studies of Government Finance sponsored by the National Committee on Government Finance. The National Committee was established in 1960 by the trustees of the Brookings Institution to supervise a comprehensive program of studies on taxation and government expenditure. The program is supported with funds provided by a grant from the Ford Foundation.

The views expressed in this study are those of the authors and conference participants and do not purport to represent the views of the Ford Foundation, the National Committee on Government Finance, the advisory committee, or the staff members, officers, or trustees of the Brookings Institution.

ROBERT D. CALKINS
President

August 1964
The Brookings Institution
1775 Massachusetts Avenue, N.W.
Washington, D.C.

Studies of Government Finance

Studies of Government Finance is a special program of research and education in taxation and government expenditures at the federal, state, and local levels. These studies are under the supervision of the National Committee on Government Finance appointed by the Trustees of the Brookings Institution, and are supported by a special grant from the Ford Foundation.

MEMBERS OF THE ADVISORY COMMITTEE

Contents

Tables

CHAPTER I

Introduction

IN THE LAST FEW YEARS, the taxation of income from foreign sources has become a controversial subject in the United States. The Revenue Act of 1962 dealt with some of the major issues, but did not completely resolve the controversy.

There are several reasons why further legislative action on taxing foreign income seems likely. Radically different approaches to the treatment of the foreign earnings of U. S. corporations and their affiliates have gained widespread support. The Kennedy Administration's 1961 proposals to restrict tax incentives for foreign investment represent one of these approaches. Others are indicated by the somewhat less restrictive, but very complicated, provisions that Congress enacted in 1962. And still others are illustrated by the Boggs Bill passed in 1960 by the House of Representatives in somewhat diluted form which would have increased, rather than decreased, incentives to export and to invest in foreign countries.

In its 1961 tax proposals, the Kennedy Administration stressed both equity and neutrality issues. That is, it not only sought legislation which would assure equal treatment of taxpayers who are similarly situated, it also had, as an objective, tax legislation that would be neutral in its effect on corporate investment plans and economic decision making generally.

In addition to these twin goals, the 1962 legislation explicitly attempted to improve the balance-of-payments position of the

1

United States. This attempt raises a number of questions. Few would dispute the proposition that, as far as possible, tax legislation should promote the foreign economic and foreign political objectives of the United States. But a number may question whether it is appropriate or possible to regulate the balance of payments through tax legislation. The current balance-of-payments deficit is an economic phenomenon of unknown duration; it will require different solutions at different times. However, it must be recognized that any tax rules for foreign-source income affect the balance of payments, regardless of intent.

Although less important than the attempt to improve the balance of payments, another objective of the 1961 proposals of the Kennedy Administration was the diversion of U. S. private investment from developed to less developed countries. Subsequently, the Johnson Administration proposed a credit of 30 percent for investments in less developed countries. One might question whether attempting such refined tasks as diverting investment from one country to another through a revenue statute is appropriate. Furthermore, does the suggestion of a 30 percent credit that was designed to be nonneutral undermine the principle of tax neutrality, one of the major justifications for the 1962 amendments?

The 1962 tax legislation affecting foreign income is complex and prolix precisely because it attempts to do more than merely collect revenues with reasonable equity. If the political and economic goals relevant to the legislation change, there may be further proposals on taxing foreign-source income. In these circumstances, this study is not exclusively concerned with the text of the 1962 amendments and with the problems, however numerous and difficult, of interpreting and applying these complicated statutory provisions. Instead, it will examine the role of taxes, the principal problems arising from the pre-1962 legislation, the various proposals advanced for amending the legislation, the extent to which such approaches have been investigated by Congress in the provisions of the present law, and the economic effects of the foreign-source income tax legislation. Finally, it will summarize the ways in which other countries handle this special tax problem.

This study is devoted primarily to the problems involved in giving American-controlled foreign corporations exemptions on their foreign-source income and also to the special rate applicable to certain foreign income of domestic corporations. Because the major policy questions now under public scrutiny concern the corporate income tax, the discussion will not, unless indicated, treat personal income taxes of citizens residing abroad or aliens living here.

The Role of Taxes

An analysis of the economic implications of taxing foreign-source income—or of any tax for that matter—should begin with a general review of taxation within an economy. When a government imposes a tax, it raises revenue for the government and induces a change in private economic behavior. The corporate income tax is an example of the kind of tax that results when raising revenue is the primary motive. An investment tax credit is an example of the kind of tax that results when directing private economic action is the primary motive. Or conceivably both purposes could be served if the tax raised revenue and helped achieve another goal of public policy. However, it is also possible that a tax would adequately achieve its primary goal but would create other undesirable consequences.

The value of a particular tax depends on how well it achieves its primary purpose, on how few unfavorable side effects it may engender, and on a third consideration—equity. An ideal revenue tax, therefore, would provide money for the government, would be neutral in its consequences for the private economy, and equitable among taxpayers.

If the two economic effects of a tax conflict, fiscal considerations presumably should be deemed more important. This presumption arises from considering what instruments are most efficient for various public goals. This conclusion is reinforced by considerations of tax equity. Raising revenue is one of the most difficult public policy goals because there are so few instruments available to achieve it. Except for taxes, the only way a government can effectively divert purchasing power from private to public uses is by selling services or goods at a profit to the private sector. Profit making by government in the United States seems unlikely because public goods are not marketable in a capitalist economy. Thus the government must depend primarily on taxes for revenue.

With the exception of the fiscal goal, there are few, if any, public goals for which the income tax mechanism is the sole instrument, or theoretically the most desirable one. This is certainly true for goals involving the foreign sector of the economy—such as protecting a domestic industry against foreign competition or strengthening the balance of payments. Furthermore, using the income tax mechanism for anything except revenue implies changing economic behavior from what it would have been without the tax. This, in turn, implies the offer of either a tax inducement or a tax penalty for private action. Because, in most cases, such inducements or penalties suggest a movement away from tax equity, they are undesirable.

Further considerations affect the selection of a proper instrument. If the goals of public policy change from time to time, the instruments employed to achieve these goals should be flexible enough to cope with such shifts. For goals likely to change in a period of one or two years, the tax mechanism is not very useful, if for no other reason than it takes longer than that to make a major legislative change in the U. S. tax laws.

Problems Leading to the 1962 Legislative Changes

Interest in how the United States taxes foreign-source income grew from a desire to affect public goals other than raising governmental revenue. The motivation for changing a long-standing tax practice stemmed mainly, as already indicated, from a desire to improve tax equity and neutrality and from the balance-of-payments difficulties the United States has experienced since 1958.

The need for strengthening the balance of payments without depressing the domestic economy, jeopardizing liberal trading principles, or weakening the international position of the dollar posed a difficult problem for American policy makers. Currency depreciation, trade restrictions, and monetary and fiscal restraint all conflicted with the needs of policy. However, the administration's analysts did not think that changes in the method of taxing foreign-source income earned in developed countries would conflict with other policy goals. The Kennedy Administration endorsed such changes since they seemed to promise an improvement in the balance of payments by discouraging foreign investment. Attention in 1961 was concentrated on direct, as distinct from portfolio, foreign investment because it seemed more amenable to policy actions. The Kennedy Administration subsequently proposed a tax limiting foreign portfolio investments.

The administration did not decide to discourage foreign investment by accident. One way in which the recent period of U. S.

TABLE 1. Private Capital Outflows from the United States by Direct and Portfolio Investment, 1950–1963[a]

(Millions of dollars)

Item	1950–55 Average	1956	1957	1958	1959	1960	1961	1962	1963
Direct investment									
U. S. to Europe	67	488	287	190	484	962	724	867	869
U. S. to other areas	634	1463	2155	991	888	712	875	787	993
Total	701	1951	2442	1181	1372	1674	1599	1654	1862
Portfolio and other investment									
U. S. to Europe	25	114	70	176	150	141	375	262	744
U. S. to other areas	229	489	789	1268	776	722	650	965	900
Total	254	603	859	1444	926	863	1025	1227	1644

Sources: U. S. Department of Commerce, *Survey of Current Business*, Vol. 44 (June 1964); U. S. Department of Commerce, *Balance of Payments, Statistical Supplement*, revised ed. (1963).
[a] All figures represent differences between new outflows and liquidations.

balance-of-payments weakness differs from previous periods of equilibrium or surplus is the substantial increase in the amount of private long-term capital outflow since 1956 (see Table 1). While the increase in the outflows of 1956 and 1957 was attributed, possibly incorrectly, to the Suez crisis, the major increases in direct investment since 1958 have been going into manufacturing facilities in Europe. This outflow cannot still be considered a temporary phenomenon; it appears to be of a more permanent nature.

In addition to concern over the balance of payments, some policy makers felt that the existing methods of taxing foreign-source income were neither neutral with respect to certain economic decisions nor equitable among taxpayers. They believed that, to be consistent with the major public policy goals, a tax change not only had to promise to reduce the balance-of-payments costs of foreign investment, it also had to improve, or at least not aggravate, the neutrality and equity of the tax, and not reverse liberal international policies.

The liberal international philosophy that the United States has professed since the end of World War II requires that the international flow of goods and capital be as free of artificial barriers as possible. The proposed tax change, therefore, must not raise a barrier restricting the flow of international capital. But the change could be endorsed if it merely tended to remove an existing artificial stimulus to such capital movements. The distinction is more than semantic. Economic theory suggests that the artificial barrier decreases world welfare (considered apart from national welfare), while removal of the artificial stimulus increases world welfare. If the change in the tax law improved both the balance of payments and tax neutrality, the change would be desirable from the standpoint of world welfare. It might also increase domestic investment and add to government revenues by closing a "loophole"—both desirable goals themselves.

The Basic Tax System for Foreign-Source Income

At the outset, it is helpful to understand the general tax provisions affecting foreign income. The 1962 amendments did not change the basic structure of the system. Instead they created another layer of exceptions and qualifications. What immediately follows summarizes how the United States treated various types of foreign income by using such mechanisms as deferral, special rates, and foreign tax credits before 1962.

U. S. Jurisdiction Over Foreign-Source Income

The United States makes one basic jurisdictional distinction in taxing corporations, and the controversial question of deferring taxes on foreign-source income is directly related to this principle of jurisdiction. Domestic corporations are taxed on their world-wide income; foreign corporations are taxed only on their income earned in the United States. A domestic corporation is defined simply as one incorporated within the United States; a foreign corporation is one incorporated outside the United States. (See Appendix B for tests of corporate nationality or residence used by other countries.) For example, if a domestic corporation operates directly in a foreign country, such a practice is usually called operating through a "branch" and it is subject to U. S. taxation on the income derived from the foreign source. If, however, a domestic corporation chooses to conduct its foreign business through a subsidiary incorporated in a foreign country, that subsidiary's foreign-source income is exempt from U. S. taxation. Although perhaps owned wholly by its U. S. parent, the subsidiary, for U. S. tax purposes, is treated as a foreign corporation wholly owned by foreign interests.

By operating through a foreign subsidiary, a U. S. enterprise can avoid any U. S. tax on the profits derived from the foreign operations until these profits are repatriated to the United States. Indeed, even on repatriation, the profits are not taxed as such. Instead, they are treated as some form of receipt to the parent corporation, the exact nature depending on whether they are repatriated as a dividend, as a distribution in liquidation, or as some other form. It is this aspect of taxing U. S. business operations abroad that is often referred to as deferral.

Western Hemisphere Trade Corporations

Quite aside from deferral, certain kinds of income from foreign operations are entitled to special tax rates. Thus, a domestic corporation qualifying under 1942 legislation as a Western Hemisphere Trade Corporation (WHTC) is entitled to a special deduction. This reduces the average effective rate of corporate income tax from about 48 percent to 34 percent.[1] To qualify as a WHTC,

---

[1] A WHTC is entitled to a deduction which is calculated by multiplying 14/48 (14 percent divided by the sum of the normal tax rate, 22 percent, and the surtax rate, 26 percent) times the taxable income computed without regard to such deduction. No corporation pays at exactly the 48 percent rate, since the surtax of 26 percent is

the domestic corporation must, in general, conduct all of its business (other than incidental purchases) in the Western Hemisphere, derive at least 95 percent of its gross income from sources outside the United States, and derive at least 90 percent of its gross income from "the active conduct of a trade or business." This third requirement disqualifies any corporation which derives more than 10 percent of its income from portfolio investment. Although the WHTC provisions were added to the Code primarily to help maintain the U. S. ownership of foreign investment and possibly to encourage new private foreign investment, they have been used principally in export operations.

Foreign Tax Credit: Direct and Derivative

Another mechanism which reduces the effective U. S. tax rate on the foreign-source income of domestic corporations is the direct foreign tax credit. Credits help corporations partially to avoid the double taxation that may occur when both the United States and the country in which the income is earned tax the foreign-source income of U. S. corporations. The credit mechanism permits the domestic corporation to deduct the amount of foreign income taxes it has paid from the U. S. tax otherwise due. Thus, the result is analogous to a dollar-for-dollar reduction in U. S. taxes.[2]

This direct credit is available only for foreign taxes paid by the taxpayer. However, the U. S. Code also provides for a derivative credit for foreign income taxes paid by the foreign subsidiaries of domestic corporations. In addition, a credit is permitted with respect to foreign income taxes "deemed to have been paid." This permits a credit for foreign taxes paid by a foreign subsidiary of the domestic corporations' foreign subsidiary. The derivative credit is taken at the time the earnings of the foreign subsidiary are distrib-

---

applicable only to taxable income in excess of $25,000. Therefore, no WHTC pays quite the 34 percent rate. This calculation was altered somewhat by the Revenue Act of 1964, which reduced the maximum corporate profits tax rate from 52 percent to 48 percent in two steps. The calculation as shown is applicable after the second step becomes operative in 1965.

[2] Because the credit is allowed, the 85 percent dividend-received deduction applicable to intercorporate dividends between domestic corporations is not available for dividends from foreign corporations.

uted as dividends to the domestic parent. Because of the method of calculating the derivative credit, employed before the Revenue Act of 1962 on income from all foreign countries, use of a foreign subsidiary provided a tax advantage in addition to deferral. Thus, the overall effective rate was lower on the earnings of a foreign subsidiary (assuming a foreign rate lower than the U. S. rate) than on the earnings of a branch of the American company, even though all of the subsidiary's earnings were distributed to the parent as dividends.[3] The old method of calculating the derivative credit is still used on earnings of foreign subsidiaries in less developed countries.

[3] This statement assumes that the foreign jurisdiction calculates taxable income in the same manner as the United States. Where a deduction is permitted under U. S. law which is not available in the foreign jurisdiction—such as the depletion allowance —the branch may prove more advantageous than the foreign subsidiary.

CHAPTER II

Problems and Alternative Solutions

CONSIDERING THE DIVERSITY of U. S. enterprises and the environments in which they are undertaken throughout the world, it would be difficult to enact equitable legislation taxing foreign-source income if the only purpose were to raise governmental revenue. When tax laws are also aimed at other goals of public policy, the problems and choices for coping with them are compounded.

The government faces at least six principal problems in taxing foreign income. The first four of these concern a single issue—the system to be adopted for taxing the income. The problems are:

1. The deferral of taxes on foreign corporate earnings until the income is sent to the United States.

2. "Tax-haven" operations in which a U. S. corporation establishes a subsidiary in a country with little or no tax on foreign-source income to use as a base company for operations in a third country.

3. Unreasonable accumulations of profits in foreign countries causing undue delay in repatriating funds subject to U. S. taxation.

4. Liquidating foreign operations, so that repatriated incomes become subject to the lower capital gains rates.

5. Making the proper allocation of income between the parent and its foreign subsidiary to obtain the greatest tax advantages. This problem arises no matter what system for taxing foreign income is adopted.

6. Deciding whether the tax rate on foreign-source income should apply universally or discriminate in favor of earnings from selected countries.

10

Proposals for taxing foreign-source income advanced by responsible critics may be divided roughly into two categories. The first, which receives major attention, concerns deferral of taxes and involves most of the problems of developing an equitable and neutral tax system. The second, which until recently has been discussed infrequently, is concerned with special tax rates to be applied to foreign-source income. An analysis of proposed solutions for each of the main problems enables us to evaluate any specific proposal.

Deferral of Taxes

Deferral of taxes on foreign-source income is important for three reasons: First, if it creates an incentive to make foreign investment at the expense of U. S. exports and investment in the United States, it departs from standards of tax neutrality. Second, if it causes an undesirable outflow of capital, it may seriously weaken the U. S. balance of payments. And third, if it delays repatriation of earnings, it might reduce total tax revenues by as much as $230 million annually.[1] Proposals for tax deferral range from eliminating it to extending it to branches of domestic corporations.

The proposals that would expand the asserted tax jurisdiction of the United States the most are those which replace the deferral provision with a current tax on the income of American-controlled foreign corporations. Although the tax might be imposed on either the foreign corporation or the U. S. shareholders, collecting it from U. S. shareholders is more feasible administratively and avoids possible conflicts with international tax treaties. It is generally conceded that the United States has no reasonable claim to a tax on that portion of a foreign corporation's foreign-source income allocable to foreign shareholders, even though U. S. shareholders control the foreign corporation. Taxing the percentage of the foreign corporation's foreign-source income which represents the proportional interest of U. S. shareholders is sufficient to eliminate deferral. One argument against this proposal is that it would be unfair to tax income which the shareholder has not received. This argument is somewhat disingenuous, however, in cases where the U. S. share-

[1] See *Revenue Act of 1962*, Report of the Senate Committee on Finance, S. Rept. 1881, 87 Cong. 2 sess. (1962), p. 393.

holders exercise control. The unfairness argument has more force when the U. S. shareholders have no connection with one another. Then, although theoretically having joint control, they may have sufficiently diverse interests so that at least some of them have no effect on corporate policy. More precisely, one shareholder may be required to pay a tax even though he has neither the funds to pay nor the power to force a dividend. Such a shareholder would be particularly wronged if he acquired his stock before Congress eliminated deferral.[2]

There must be a clear definition of control if the tax is to be limited to situations where U. S. shareholders are jointly able to exercise this control. It seems preferable to limit the tax to situations where U. S. shareholders hold more than 50 percent of the outstanding voting stock, even though holders of relatively low percentages of voting stock may have actual control.

The desire to enable particular U. S. taxpayers to determine with some certainty whether the requisite percentage of U. S. ownership exists creates problems of definition. Moreover, so that the U. S. tax is not easily avoided, it is necessary to apply attribution rules to determine U. S. stock ownership—attributing ownership, say, as between husband and wife. Requiring U. S. taxpayers to determine what other U. S. shareholders a foreign corporation has may be a burden; but requiring them to determine what is considered an American-controlled corporation according to the attributions rules of the statutory definition is doubly burdensome. Such problems of definition may be lessened in two ways: First, only those U. S. shareholders who own at least a certain percentage would be counted. Second, the foreign corporation would be considered American-controlled only when a limited number of U. S. shareholders (for example, five or less) hold, directly or indirectly, more than 50 percent of the outstanding stock. It might be observed that the foreign personal holding company provisions of the Internal Revenue Code have created similar problems of definition, and well-advised taxpayers apparently have adjusted their affairs to avoid the penalties of the holding company provisions.

If it is possible to remove the disparity in treatment between

---

[2] Unfairness to a single stockholder is discussed further in Appendix A.

branches and foreign subsidiaries by eliminating the deferral advantage of the foreign subsidiary, with equal logic the difference can be eliminated by extending the advantage to foreign branches of domestic corporations. Such a proposal would, of course, require domestic corporations to keep separate accounts for foreign branches, and it would raise allocation problems concerning the price of transferring goods between domestic and foreign branches of the same corporation. Moreover, the percentage depletion allowance presumably would thereby also be denied to the foreign-source income of extractive enterprises. Since most oil companies find it advantageous to operate branches rather than foreign subsidiaries abroad,[3] at least some enterprises would probably be affected adversely by the extension of foreign subsidiary treatment to branches. But giving the taxpayer the option of treating his branch as a subsidiary for extractive enterprises could avoid such adverse consequences.

Tax-Haven Operations

The problems involved in tax-haven operations of U. S. business enterprises are closely related to those of tax deferral for foreign subsidiaries. The Treasury was concerned about the growing use of certain third-country arrangements—the so-called tax-haven operations—used to obtain substantial tax advantages made possible by the deferral mechanism. Many subsidiaries of U. S. enterprises have been incorporated in countries without any intent to conduct business there. Instead, these subsidiaries are established in countries where taxes on foreign-source income are low, or even non-existent, in order to operate in third countries—either directly or through "grandchild" subsidiaries. For convenience, throughout this study the country of incorporation is called the "base country," and the country in which the business is conducted is labeled the "country of operations" or the "country of destination," depending on whether it manufactures abroad or exports from the United States. If the base company manufactures abroad, it may function

---

[3] See discussion by Walter W. Brudno, "Review of Considerations Arising in Foreign Oil Operations," Institute on Oil and Gas Law and Taxation as It Affects the Oil and Gas Industry, *Proceedings of the Ninth Annual Institute* (Matthew Bender & Co., 1958), pp. 397–460.

in the country of operations through either its branches or local subsidiaries.[4] When a U. S. manufacturer establishes a base company to handle its export sales from the United States, the base company normally will operate in one of two ways. It will operate through a branch located in the country to which goods are destined; or it will seek through principal-to-principal selling arrangements to avoid any direct contact with the country where the sales are made.

A base company may also perform services abroad for its U. S. parent or for another foreign subsidiary. Base companies that perform selling services in support of the parent's export operations and those that perform management services in connection with foreign manufacturing operations have been particularly significant. Such companies are also used in licensing foreign patents, copyrights, trade-marks, and so on that are developed by the U. S. parent or related corporations.

While it was held, both within the administration and without, that there was a tax-haven problem that differed from, or that transcended, the deferral problem, the grounds for distinguishing between the two are far from clear. In much of the recent discussion, it has been assumed that base companies are frequently used to avoid U. S. taxes. In fact, it is the deferral mechanism which permits the parent corporation to avoid U. S. taxes in normal base-company arrangements. To put the proposition differently: as long as deferral exists, it will be unusual if use of a base company permits income to escape U. S. taxation which otherwise would have been subject to such taxation. Three examples of typical base company arrangements—one of an export business and two of foreign manufacturing operations—may serve as illustrations.

1. Assume that a U. S. corporation engaged in exporting goods from the United States uses a base company as part of an arrangement to "move" the sales profits beyond the reach of the U. S. tax. In such a case, it is—strictly speaking—the deferral mechanism, and not the use of the base company, which permits the exemption from U. S. taxation. The same result, from the standpoint of U. S.

[4] To the extent that the base company operates through a local subsidiary, it is a holding company, and the base company may be organized in a country that exempts dividend income from foreign subsidiaries, whether it exempts other classes of foreign-source income.

taxes, could have been achieved by organizing a subsidiary directly held by the U. S. parent in the country of destination.

2. Similarly, if a base company's branch manufactures in the country of operations, it is the deferral mechanism that produces the desired U. S. tax result. Again, the same U. S. tax result could have been achieved by carrying out the manufacturing through a subsidiary organized in the country of operations and held directly by the U. S. parent.

3. Where manufacturing is conducted by a local subsidiary organized in the country of operations and the stock of that local operating subsidiary is held by a base company, the insertion of the base company as an intermediary does not produce any additional saving in U. S. taxes.[5]

Saying that the use of base companies does not cause any greater avoidance of U. S. tax than is inherent in the deferral mechanism should not suggest, however, that the use of base companies provides no advantages. On the contrary, the widespread use of base companies underscores their dramatic advantages. But these advantages involve either the avoidance of the taxes of foreign countries or considerations not related to taxes. Thus, in the first example, a U. S. corporation involved in exporting, the suggested alternative of incorporating a local subsidiary in the country of destination, could have caused a substantial increase in the payment of local taxes. By using a base company, a parent may escape taxation in the country of destination while it retains the deferral advantage and, at the same time, incurs little or no tax liability in the country

[5] It is true that where several foreign operating companies are involved, the use of a base holding company may permit capital transfers from one operating company to another without subjecting the U. S. parent to taxation on a constructive dividend theory. Since the funds are at no time within the immediate possession of the U. S. parent, there is no basis to infer that a dividend has been paid. The same U. S. tax result could have been achieved, however, through alternative corporate arrangements not involving base companies, such as making the transferee operating company a subsidiary of the transferrer, or vice versa. Use of a base company may also be of some limited utility in permitting U. S. parent corporations to avoid loss of potential derivative foreign tax credits where the per country limitation is applicable—that is, the aggregation of earnings and taxes paid is not allowed. Through use of a base company, it is possible, in effect, to average foreign tax rates applicable in various foreign countries. These matters, which are beyond the scope of this paper, have been of limited import since a 1960 amendment that permitted taxpayers to elect the overall limitation subject to certain minor restrictions.

in which the base company is incorporated. In the second example, precisely the same avoidance of foreign taxes is the principal advantage of using a base company to conduct a foreign manufacturing operation. In the third illustration, using a base holding company permits certain advantages unrelated to taxes. For example, risks of expropriation by the country of operations and of devaluation of that country's currency may be partially avoided by declaring dividends to an intermediate base company.

Such action, of course, must be coupled with removal of the funds from the jurisdiction and conversion to a more stable currency. Converting funds to another currency without declaring a dividend might avoid the risk of devaluation. But when a substantial exchange risk exists, an exchange licensing system may well deny local companies the privilege of acquiring foreign exchange. In such a situation, a dividend may be the only feasible method of converting to a sounder currency.

Assuming deferral is desirable as a matter of U. S. tax policy, one may still question whether any effort should be made to restrict the use of base companies. There is no obvious reason the United States should object to base companies used simply to avoid the taxes of other countries or to gain certain nontax advantages. However, the general criticism of base-company operations is understandable. Even if the base company has no significance in the day-to-day business operations of an enterprise, the triumph of form over substance may offend one's sense of tax propriety. Certainly the widespread use of base companies creates resentment against the deferral mechanism.

The Kennedy Administration's principal argument against base companies appeared to be that, coupled with deferral, avoiding foreign taxes creates a situation in which the overall effective tax rate, domestic and foreign, is comparatively low. Such a rate can be so low that a substantial preference for foreign over domestic investment can be created, possibly straining the U. S. balance of payments.[6] According to this view, legislating against tax havens, although less satisfactory than eliminating deferral, tends to minimize the artificial incentive to foreign investment, reduces the

---

[6] See, for example, the *President's 1961 Tax Recommendations*, Hearings before the House Ways and Means Committee, 87 Cong. 1 sess. (1961), Vol. 1, p. 30.

impact of foreign investment on the balance of payments, and moderates the loss in revenue—all of which the administration felt were the main undesirable consequences of deferral. Nevertheless, an attempt to restrict the use of base companies, without challenging deferral, is necessarily a rather undiscriminating limitation on deferral. Even if a corporation's use of base companies is restricted, it can continue to secure the benefits of deferral, but will lose certain additional benefits, such as the ability to avoid foreign taxes or to protect against nontax risks, for example, expropriation and devaluation.

Even if the base company is considered primarily a device for avoiding foreign taxes, it is quite proper to ask whether the United States does not in some situations have an interest in helping other countries to avoid the resulting drain on their revenues. Certainly, the countries whose taxes are being avoided should be primarily responsible for protecting their own revenues. Thus, a base company in Panama may be used to avoid taxes in a South American country to which the U. S. enterprise is exporting. If so, it might be argued that, by changing its rules governing source of income, the South American country can sweep the profits of the Panamanian base company within its taxing jurisdiction. Panama could not persuasively object to such action by the importing country because Panama does not seek to tax those profits. At least as long as the base company does not operate extensively in Panama, the financial interest of Panama in securing Panamanian incorporation provides little basis for such an objection.

Since separating the problem of deferral from that of the tax haven is difficult, it is not easy to construct a statutory definition which will isolate the tax-haven virus for treatment. Theoretically, the principal defined concept could be the tax-haven company, with all of its income taxed under special rules. Or legislation might be based on the tax-haven transaction, the income from which would be taxed specially without regard to the percentage of gross or net income represented by such transactions.

A definition of a tax-haven company apparently must include two related identifying elements. A first test is that an American-controlled business must be conducted in one foreign country through a company incorporated in another foreign country. A second test, requiring more judgment, is that substantial business activities must not be conducted in the country of incorporation.

The first requirement, separating the place of business from the place of incorporation, excludes from the tax-haven category foreign business operations conducted in countries with low income tax rates or countries granting tax holidays to foreign investors. Inherent in the concept of deferral is the sovereignty of each country over the effective overall tax rate to be applied to local corporations operating within the country.

The second requirement—that substantial business activities not be conducted in the country of incorporation—would avoid imposing a strait jacket, which would certainly result if a separate subsidiary had to be incorporated for each country in which business was conducted. There are many legitimate nontax considerations which may induce enterprises not to incorporate in every country in which they manufacture or sell. For example, an enterprise might have plants in the six countries of the European Economic Community (EEC). But it might choose on the basis of nontax considerations to incorporate in only one. As long as substantial business operations are conducted in the country of incorporation, the United States could not reasonably take the position that the incorporation had only a tax motive. In drafting statutory language on this second requirement, the need to promote certainty in tax planning may well dictate the construction of more elaborate factual tests to determine what constitutes substantial business operations in the country of incorporation.

If a definition of a tax-haven transaction is preferred, it would be simply the typical transaction of a tax-haven company—that is, a transaction having its locus outside the country of incorporation. One might add a requirement that the country of incorporation exempt from taxation the income from such transactions. However, such a requirement often would be superfluous considering the general reluctance of most foreign countries to tax income from outside sources. To determine the locus of the most common transaction, traditional legal principles could be used to determine the place of sale. Or, if one feared that under such principles resourceful counsel could too easily manipulate the legal form of transactions to avoid the tax-haven provisions, other tests, such as the place of ultimate use of the goods, could be used. But whatever the standard, not every transaction with its locus outside the state of incorporation should be treated as a tax-haven transaction. The EEC example is apt, because if business considerations require a single subsidiary to handle Common Market operations, it would be unfortunate if U. S. tax law should penalize such a corporate structure. A tax-haven statute should impose a penalty only where tax considerations are a major, if not the principal, reason for separating incorporation from business activity. No matter how that drafting problem is solved, it would be desirable—in order to avoid administrative problems and too rigid limitations on choosing the place of incorporation—to provide that transactions meeting the formal indicia of tax-haven transactions be taxed only where they constitute a designated percentage of the gross or net income of the foreign corporation.

Unreasonable Accumulations

When the effective foreign tax rate is substantially below the U. S. rate, deferral of taxes on foreign-source income enables American-controlled foreign corporations to accumulate capital at a much faster rate than would otherwise be possible. This factor, coupled with the combination of the dividend taxes of the foreign country and the tax imposed by the United States on the receipt of dividends from foreign subsidiaries, may induce retention of foreign funds not currently needed for the foreign business operations, rather than repatriation of those funds. As long as the funds earn some interest—through investments in governmental securities, for example—it may be more profitable for the parent corporation not to repatriate. Thus, it may be appropriate to deny deferral to that part of retained foreign-source income which exceeds the reasonable needs of the foreign subsidiary's business. Indeed, taxing all income from portfolio or "passive" investments when it is earned may be desirable whether or not the funds may be needed in the active trade or business within the reasonable future. Denying deferral for foreign-source income derived from portfolio investment would seem especially appropriate if the U. S. balance of payments was considered of primary importance in formulating tax policy on foreign income.

One of the possible difficulties in attempting to forestall unreasonable accumulations of profits is that tax legislation, instead of inducing the repatriation of foreign earnings, may stimulate reinvestment. The U. S. Treasury might prefer to permit liquid balances to accumulate which might eventually be repatriated, rather than to induce immediate reinvestment in less liquid operating facilities in the foreign country by threatening to impose an unreasonable accumulations tax.

A closely related problem arises from what may be termed the "disguised dividend." Some U. S. parent corporations attempt to disguise as investments made by their foreign subsidiaries in the United States what are in fact dividends to the parent in order to avoid U. S. taxes on the dividends. A simple illustration would be a long-term loan by a foreign subsidiary to its parent.

Proposals to prevent the abuse of deferral through unreasonable accumulations would expand U. S. tax jurisdiction, although perhaps less than the tax-haven proposals. An amendment to limit unreasonable accumulations might take one of two forms: (1) imposing a special tax called, perhaps, a "foreign-unreasonable-accumulations tax" or (2) eliminating deferral on income that was unreasonably accumulated. The principal difference would be that the foreign-unreasonable-accumulations tax would be levied at the time of the accumulation, and another tax (the conventional income tax on dividends) would be levied at the time the earnings and profits in question were distributed. Proposals to eliminate deferral, on the contrary, normally do not provide for additional taxes on distribution because the purpose of eliminating deferral is to treat the foreign subsidiary as a branch of the U. S. parent.

Whichever amendment was adopted, the amount of profits unreasonably accumulated would have to be determined. One approach would be to separate all assets of the foreign corporation into the categories of qualified and nonqualified property. That done, the foreign-unreasonable-accumulations tax or the regular income tax would be imposed on either the additions of nonqualified property or on gross income not reinvested in qualified property. An alternate approach would be to impose the special tax on or to deny deferral to all income derived from nonqualified property.

In either case, nonqualified property would be defined to include at least all portfolio investments, such as stocks and bonds (except, perhaps, stock in foreign-operating subsidiaries of the foreign corporation to the extent of such subsidiaries' investment in qualified property). Nonqualified property might also include, in order to discourage disguised dividends to the U. S. parent, all property located in the United States (except, perhaps, certain classes of property necessary for the conduct of the trade or business of the foreign corporation). Finally, if reducing foreign investment were considered of overwhelming importance, all investments in new trades or businesses might be treated as investments in nonqualified property.

Liquidation at Capital Gains Rates

Those who support deferral frequently argue that the U. S. enterprise gains no permanent advantage because the tax on foreign-source income must always be paid at the time of repatriation. This argument can be partially refuted by pointing out some permanent advantages. First, deferral amounts to an interest-free loan from the U. S. government for the period pending payment. Second, the foreign subsidiary's profits may never be repatriated, but rather reinvested to form the permanent capital for a foreign operation. Third, the taxes paid at the time of repatriation may not be as great as the total of current taxes in the absence of deferral, even assuming no change in U. S. tax rates in the interim. The advantages from deferral may be compounded by dissolving the foreign subsidiary when repatriating. The accumulated foreign earnings would then be returned as a distribution in complete liquidation, taxable at capital gains rates, rather than as a dividend. However, the derivative credit for the subsidiary's tax payments to the foreign country is not available for such a liquidating distribution. Thus, liquidation is preferable to a dividend only when the foreign tax rate is so low (specifically, less than 23 percent where the U. S. rate is 48 percent) that the advantage of the capital gains rate outweighs the advantage of the credit.[7]

[7] In principle, a tax-free liquidation (or merger, consolidation, or reorganization) of the foreign subsidiary is possible. However, such a liquidation requires a Treasury ruling that the avoidance of federal income taxes is not a principal purpose—a ruling that the Treasury usually is unwilling to give.

Tax Incentives for Foreign Business

Despite the 1962 legislation which was aimed at dampening enthusiasm for foreign investment—except in less developed countries—there are recurring proposals for tax incentives encouraging foreign operations. Among these are the creation of special foreign business corporations, special tax rates for foreign-source income, and tax credits for investment in less developed countries. The usual proposal for special kinds of corporations is to provide tax exemption either on foreign-source income or on all income as long as the special corporation meets certain statutory standards designed to assure that its income is derived primarily from foreign operations. Such a corporation—often called a foreign business corporation (FBC)—would be expected to act as the foreign business arm of domestic enterprises. Therefore, it is sometimes proposed that the dividends to the parent also be exempt in order to give the maximum encouragement to foreign trade and investment. Without exempting dividends, such a proposal would grant FBC deferral treatment analogous to that possible under the pre-1962 law through use of a foreign subsidiary. If dividends were exempted, however, the FBC proposal would be like those for exempting foreign-source income derived from foreign branches of domestic corporations.[8]

As long as American-controlled foreign corporations are entitled to deferral, most U. S. enterprises merely would consider an FBC as an alternative to a foreign subsidiary. The FBC would have certain limited advantages, such as simplicity of organization, eligibility for benefits under U. S. tax treaties, and eligibility for United States government investment guarantees. But it might have serious disadvantages if restrictions were placed on eligibility for FBC status. Moreover, the principal advantages an FBC provision gives the Treasury—more effective administration and prevention of abuses—would be lost if deferral could also be secured through foreign subsidiary corporations. By coupling the FBC exemption to

---

[8] A slight variant of the exemption-for-dividends proposal is to grant the parent the 85 percent dividends-received deduction presently available on intercorporate dividends among domestic corporations. Under the present top corporate rate of 48 percent, the effective rate on dividends would be 7.2 percent.

the elimination of deferral, however, it might be possible to grant U. S. enterprises the principal advantages of deferral while eliminating tax-haven operations and unreasonable accumulations.

Proposals for special tax rates vary widely in purpose and method. One such proposal is represented by the provisions which permit a domestic corporation to qualify as a Western Hemisphere Trade Corporation (WHTC). But in the case of the WHTC the special rate is granted for all of the income of a corporation meeting the designated standards.

Recently, the Commerce Committee for the Alliance for Progress (COMAP) recommended that tax inducements for investment in Latin America be substantially broadened.[9] In addition to a number of nontax proposals, the following tax measures were suggested:

1. An investment tax credit of at least 25 percent on all new and additional U. S. private investment in countries of the Western Hemisphere. This suggestion has subsequently been recommended by the Johnson Administration.

2. A tax certificate permitting a minimum return of 5 percent on capital after taxes to be used by U. S. companies in selected enterprises as a credit against their U. S. income tax liability when such minimum return is not achieved.

3. A tax credit for foreign-exchange losses arising from currency devaluation.

4. Creation of a new type of corporation (Alliance for Progress Corporation), whose earnings would not be taxed until distributed to shareholders provided that earnings were reinvested in the less developed countries of the Western Hemisphere.

5. A U. S. income tax deduction for losses on foreign investment.

6. An amendment to U. S. tax law to provide for tax sparing where the host countries offer tax incentives as part of a program to attract new basic industries. Tax sparing refers to a credit against U. S. taxes for taxes foregone by the host country as part of a program to lure U. S. investment.

In determining the size and need for a preferential rate, one

[9] U. S. Department of Commerce, *Proposals to Improve the Flow of U. S Private Investment to Latin America* (March 1963).

must keep in mind the purpose of the preference. For example, if the basic purpose is to promote private foreign investment, taking steps to deny the preferential rate to export income may be desirable. If the purpose is to promote U. S. exports in order to aid the balance of payments, however, investment income should not be permitted to qualify. Experience with the WHTC provisions illustrates the consequences of failing to consider these matters. As far as can be determined from the sketchy legislative history, the purpose underlying the WHTC provisions was the maintenance and promotion of direct investment in Latin America, but the chief beneficiaries of these provisions today are exporters.

Similarly, placing geographical limitations on the source of income entitled to the preferential rate, as in the case of the WHTC provisions, may be desirable. Thus, the preferential rate might be limited to income having its source in less developed areas, if developing those areas is considered an appropriate goal of tax policy.

As long as the foreign-source income of all foreign corporations is exempt, preferential rate provisions would apply only to domestic corporations. However, it is possible to grant a preferential rate on repatriation of earnings from foreign corporations. The pre-1962 method of calculating the derivative foreign tax credit produces something like a preferential rate, although this rate varies with the rate of the foreign tax being credited. If using a preferential rate on the repatriated income of domestic corporations is desirable, it might be preferable to change the method of calculating the foreign tax credit still available on income earned in less developed countries to eliminate the irrational preference and to impose a flat reduction in rate on such income.

The part of the COMAP proposal concerning a 25 percent investment tax credit has various advantages for the investor. A credit increases the rate of return. It reduces the net cost of the investment. It reduces the cash outlay needed to acquire an asset. Some people also maintain that a credit, by returning part of the cost immediately, shortens the pay-out period, thereby reducing risk. Finally, the credit may be considered a way of lowering the effective interest rate on financing investments. The foregoing advantages were suggested by the Treasury in connection with the 7 percent investment credit for domestic corporations provided in the Revenue Act of 1962, although some differences exist between the two credits.[10] These advantages, therefore, may also be advanced in support of any credit for investment in less developed countries. While they make an impressive list, they are merely different ways of expressing the same idea.

Some major issues arise in defining the category of investments which will qualify for the credit. Should the credit be limited, as the 1962 domestic investment credit was, to tangible assets? Or should intangibles be included? Will portfolio investments and investments in debt instruments qualify? Will reinvestment qualify? If so, will it qualify only after the corresponding earnings from the old investment have in some way been subjected to U. S. taxation? If earnings from the less developed country are reinvested in a new business or a new country, will they be treated differently from reinvestment in an existing business or in the same country?

Once the type of qualifying investment is defined, a definition is needed for the type of corporation which will qualify. Should the credit be available to both domestic corporations and foreign corporations controlled by U. S. interests? Will an American-controlled foreign corporation which is not taxable on its foreign-source income qualify? If so, how will it use the credit? May a domestic parent corporation utilize a credit created by an investment made by its foreign subsidiary? Will base companies be treated specially? The answers to these questions will have a major impact on the usefulness of the credit. The proposed legislation answers some of these questions.

Another series of decisions concerns withdrawal, or sale, of investments. Some mechanism will no doubt be necessary to recoup for the Treasury part of the credit in the event of early sale or withdrawal of investment.

Questions of timing also arise. Companies must often wait some years after investing before they can reap the profits. Perhaps some carry-over mechanism will be necessary to make the credit fully effective. Alternatively, the credit would be made applicable to income wherever earned.

[10] C. Douglas Dillon, *The Revenue Act of 1962*, Hearings before the Senate Finance Committee, 87 Cong. 2 sess. (1962), Pt. 1, pp. 47–87.

One basic policy question is whether the Treasury should have some right to screen investments to select those that are to qualify. Such screening need not involve the individual licensing of investments, but might be more general. For example, the credit might be made available only for investments in countries which had previously improved the investment climate by compensating for expropriations and similar matters. An analogy is the investment guarantee program of the Agency for International Development. Such guarantees are restricted to countries which have made treaties with the United States.

Allocation of Income Within a Single Enterprise

The problem in taxing foreign-source income, which no system seems able to eliminate entirely, concerns the allocation of income among corporations within a single enterprise. So long as exemptions and special rates are available, there will be a strong incentive to arrange intra-enterprise transactions so that the maximum amount of income qualifies for the exemption or special rate. Thus, on sales between a U. S. manufacturing parent and a foreign sales subsidiary, there is a strong incentive to stipulate a price as low as possible so that not only the selling portion, but also the manufacturing portion, of the profit becomes the income of the subsidiary. Unfortunately, where buyer and seller are under common control, the discipline of the market place is not available to assure an arm's-length price.

The administration's concern with this problem of allocating income is understandable. It may be that the dominant problem under the foreign-income provisions involves allocation of income between the U. S. parent, on the one hand, and its foreign subsidiary, base company, or Western Hemisphere Trade Corporation on the other. For example, if using base companies enables the parent corporation to avoid the U. S. tax, the avoidance arises almost solely from the siphoning of domestic profits into base companies. Such avoidance perhaps could be more directly prevented by better allocation rules, or more stringent enforcement of the present allocation rules, than by the more drastic remedy of attempting to eliminate tax havens.

CHAPTER III

Legislative Choices Among Alternative Proposals

THE EMPHASIS NOW SHIFTS from an analysis of the problems and alternative solutions to a more factual description of the history of tax legislation on foreign-source income, particularly the 1962 amendments. In doing so, the main purpose is to determine how fully the various schemes for taxing foreign income have been considered and adopted.

Developments Before 1960

The modern corporate income tax dates from 1909.[1] Under the 1909 statute, domestic corporations were taxed on income "from all sources" and foreign corporations on income from "business transacted and capital invested within the United States."[2] This jurisdictional pattern, which remained substantially unchanged until 1962, does not appear to have been the subject of discussion at the time of enactment either in committee or on the floor. Doubtless the low rate of only 1 percent made the question of tax-

[1] Prototypes of the corporate tax were contained in the 1870 and 1894 acts. Jacob Stewart Seidman, *Legislative History of Federal Income Tax Laws, 1938–1961* (Prentice-Hall, 1938), pp. 1016–26.

[2] 36 Stat. 11, 61 Cong. 1 sess. (1909).

ing the income of foreign corporations controlled by U. S. interests insignificant, if, indeed, anyone gave consideration to treating such foreign corporations differently from other foreign corporations.

The impact of the tax on the foreign-source income of domestic corporations was softened somewhat in 1918 by the adoption of a foreign tax credit.[3] Previously foreign taxes had merely been deductible, like state and local taxes.[4] There is little legislative history. The only witness at the hearings to address himself to the question urged exemption of foreign-source income, or at least a lower rate for such income. He pointed to the double taxation involved in paying both foreign and U. S. taxes and the difficulty in competing with foreign firms which, because their countries did not tax foreign-source income, were subject to tax only in the source jurisdiction.[5] The chairman of the House Ways and Means Committee indicated in the course of the hearings that the introduction of a foreign tax credit would be an appropriate compromise.[6] Thus, on the basis of the scanty record, apparently the Congress as early as 1918 determined that the foreign-source income of domestic corporations was only entitled to limited special treatment in the form of the credit.

In 1921, a further attempt was made to exempt the foreign-source income of domestic corporations. The House passed a provision that would have created a special class of foreign trade corporation exempt from taxation on foreign-source income. The proposal failed in the Senate, however, under the determined opposition of Senator Robert LaFollette.[7]

In 1942, the Western Hemisphere Trade Corporation (WHTC) provisions were adopted. Despite the meager legislative history, Congress clearly thought the purpose was to place domestic enterprises doing business in Latin America on a better competitive

---

[3] Revenue Act of 1918, Sec. 222, 65 Cong. 3 sess. (1918), 40 Stat. 1057.

[4] House Ways and Means Committee, *Revenue Bill of 1918*, H. Rept. 767, 65 Cong. 2 sess. (1918).

[5] Statement of John J. Shea, *Revenue Act of 1918*, Hearings before the House Ways and Means Committee, 65 Cong. 2 sess., Vol. 1 (1918), pp. 442–57.

[6] *Ibid.*, pp. 445–47.

[7] *Congressional Record*, Vol. 61 (1921), pp. 6548–49. See discussion at pp. 5878, 5883–86, 6489–94, 6540–49, 6573–74, 7228–29.

footing with foreign enterprises.[8] There is some basis for concluding that Congress primarily aimed at aid to manufacturing, mining, and utility operations, instead of providing aid to exports,[9] but, as noted earlier, the provisions have helped the latter.

During the 1950's, various bills exempting foreign-source income or lowering the applicable rate were introduced, but all were sidetracked or defeated—including the 1954 Internal Revenue Code in the form originally passed by the House. Perhaps most important was the Boggs bill. As originally introduced in 1959, it provided essentially for extending WHTC treatment to world-wide operations and creating a new tax entity, a foreign business corporation (FBC). The House Ways and Means Committee dropped the former provisions, but the FBC provisions—in sharply limited form— were passed by the House. The bill failed to emerge from the Senate Finance Committee before the adjournment of the Eighty-sixth Congress in 1960. In the bill passed by the House, FBC status was limited to domestic corporations deriving at least 90 percent of gross income from the active conduct of a trade or business (thus excluding portfolio investment income) and conducting substantially all of their business in less developed countries.[10]

Thus, before the Kennedy Administration, no major changes in the tax law governing taxation of foreign income had been made since the WHTC enactment of 1942. But the rise of balance-of-payments problems for the United States, coupled with a movement toward tax reform, culminated in President Kennedy's 1961 proposal to eliminate deferral.

[8] Senate Finance Committee, *Revenue Bill of 1942*, S. Rept. 1631, 77 Cong. 2 sess. (1942), p. 32.

[9] See Hearings before the Senate Finance Committee, 77 Cong. 2 sess. (1942), pp. 1204–10, 2273–76; Senate Finance Committee, S. Rept. 1631, cited above, p. 111. See also Stanley S. Surrey, "Current Issues in the Taxation of Corporate Foreign Income," 56 Columbia L. Rev. 815, 834–36.

[10] Further limitations were that the foreign business corporation must not have derived more than 10 percent of gross income from sale of articles for ultimate use, consumption, or disposition in the United States, and must not have been operated under substandard labor conditions as determined by the Secretary of Labor. *Congressional Record*, Vol. 106 (1960), pp. 9815–28 (daily ed. May 18, 1960). See David R. Tillinghast, "Taxation of Foreign Income: A Critique of the Boggs Bill," 16 Tax L. Rev. 81 (1960).

The Kennedy Administration's 1961 Proposals

On April 20, 1961, President Kennedy delivered to Congress a message proposing, among other changes in the tax law, the complete elimination of deferral.[11] The President's recommendation was amplified by Secretary of the Treasury C. Douglas Dillon in testimony before the House Ways and Means Committee on May 3, 1961, and in a "Detailed Explanation of the President's Recommendations" filed with the committee at that time.[12] The "Detailed Explanation" set forth the proposed changes in narrative form; and the House Ways and Means Committee hearings were held without benefit of any draft statutory language.

After the hearings, it became apparent that the committee was not interested in a bill which went so far as to eliminate deferral. The Treasury, therefore, released on July 28, 1961, a draft of proposed legislation designed to discourage tax-haven operations and "passive" investments (stocks, bonds, and so on) while generally preserving the deferral mechanism. A revised Treasury draft on tax havens, released on January 31, 1962, was followed on February 1 by a press release from the Committee on Ways and Means proposing a still more modest approach—essentially a bill to deal with unreasonable accumulations.

On February 27, the committee issued another press release indicating a return to a combined tax-haven and unreasonable-accumulations approach. As spelled out in H.R. 10650 in the form passed by the House of Representatives on March 29, U. S. shareholders with an interest of 10 percent or greater in an American-controlled foreign corporation were to be taxed on certain undistributed earnings of the foreign corporation. Such shareholders would be taxed on that portion of the undistributed earnings representing certain defined classes of tax-haven income; and, in addition, on the remaining undistributed earnings not reinvested in certain types of qualified property. In one significant respect H.R. 10650 went beyond a tax-haven measure. One premise of the ex-

[11] *President's 1961 Tax Recommendations*, Hearings before the House Ways and Means Committee, 87 Cong. 1 sess. (1961), pp. 3, 8–10.
[12] *Ibid.*, pp. 260–65, 301 ff.

ception for qualified property was that legitimate manufacturing operations should not be penalized in an attempt to root out tax-haven operations. But under an "anti-diversification" provision of the House bill, the concept of qualified property was limited so that investment in new manufacturing facilities would not constitute qualified property. This limitation partially eliminated deferral, even when no tax-haven operations were involved.

Following passage of the bill by the House, hearings began almost immediately before the Senate Finance Committee. For one month, a parade of witnesses—almost all hostile to the proposed legislation—appeared before the committee. These witnesses pointed out numerous inequities and technical deficiencies in the House bill. Secretary Dillon then appeared before the committee on May 10 to propose certain changes in the bill. He said the Treasury's formal position continued to be that "elimination of deferral for operations in developed countries would be the most equitable and appropriate policy," and he made clear that his changes were proposed only if "the committee [should] decide to adopt an approach along the lines of the House bill" and that the "suggestions for such changes should not be taken as indicating any lessening of our support for the elimination of deferral."[13] Nonetheless the Treasury draft encompassing the changes, which was released on May 31, became the basis for the Senate Finance Committee's work. The most important of the changes was that the "anti-diversification" provision was deleted, so that an investment in new manufacturing or other facilities would not increase the tax payable by the shareholder, provided the investment was not in property situated in the United States.

Following additional hearings, the Senate committee on August 16 reported out a bill which adopted substantially the Treasury draft of May 31, subject to two major additions, a minimum distribution provision and an export trade corporation provision.[14] The bill was passed without major changes by the Senate, approved by the Conference Committee, and signed by the President.

The President's recommendations to Congress in 1961 did not

---

[13] *Revenue Act of 1962*, Hearings before the Senate Finance Committee, Pt. 10, 87 Cong. 2 sess., pp. 4252–53.

[14] Senate Finance Committee, *Revenue Act of 1962*, S. Rept. 1881, 87 Cong. 2 sess.

contain any reference to an allocation-of-income provision—presumably because if deferral were to be completely eliminated, the allocation-of-income problem would largely disappear.[15] But when complete elimination of deferral was found unacceptable by the House Ways and Means Committee, the problem reasserted itself and a special provision for it was drafted. The House bill would have revised Section 482 to add a subsection permitting the Treasury, based on a special formula, to allocate the taxable income (rather than gross income, deductions, credits, and allowances as under the existing version of Section 482) arising from sales of tangible property among related entities. The formula was based on assets, payroll, and distribution expenses of the respective entities, except when the taxpayer could establish an arm's-length price on the basis of similar transactions with unrelated entities. The Senate Finance Committee removed the allocation provision entirely and this action was upheld by the Conference Committee, apparently because it was too difficult to draft a workable formula that improved the existing statutory provisions without being unduly restrictive and inflexible. The rejection of the proposed solution to the allocation problem is somewhat anomalous in view of the urging of some business groups that, if a tax-haven problem did exist, it could be solved solely by strengthening the Section 482 allocation provision. The suggestion by the Conference Committee that the Treasury should promulgate additional allocation regulations, if viewed as more than buck-passing, may constitute a legislative judgment that at least some foreign-income problems might be better handled by administrative action than by legislation. The suggestion in full reads:

The conferees on the part of both the House and the Senate believe that the objectives of section 6 of the bill as passed by the House can be accomplished by amendment of the regulations under present section 482. Section 482 already contains broad authority to the Secretary of the Treasury or his delegate to allocate income and deductions. It is believed that the Treasury should explore the possibility of developing and promulgating regulations under this authority which would provide additional guidelines

---

[15] The allocation of income problem would remain on transactions between a manufacturing parent and a WHTC subsidiary, but that situation was largely outside the scope of the proposed legislation.

and formulas for the allocation of income and deductions in cases involving foreign income.[16]

1962 Action on Deferral and Tax Havens

The Revenue Act of 1962 eliminated the deferral of the U. S. tax on certain categories of income made by "controlled foreign corporations." A controlled foreign corporation is defined as a foreign corporation with more than 50 percent of its voting power owned by U. S. shareholders, each owning at least 10 percent of that voting power. Each U. S. shareholder possessing a 10 percent interest in an American-controlled foreign corporation is required to include in gross income his pro rata share of the foreign corporation's "foreign base-company income," which is the income from certain types of transactions reduced "so as to take into account deductions (including taxes) properly allocable to such income." Thus, the technique of defining tax-haven transactions, rather than defining a tax-haven company, was adopted to avoid the difficulty mentioned previously of differentiating between tax-haven abuses and legitimate benefits of deferral.

The resulting definition of foreign base-company income, while extremely complex, may be summarized as follows: foreign base-company income includes (1) foreign personal holding company income (in general, dividends, interest, royalties, and rents); (2) foreign base-company sales income (in general, income derived from the purchase and sale of personal property where the purchase is from, or the sale to, a related person and where the property purchased is "manufactured, produced, grown, or extracted outside," and "sold for use, consumption, or disposition outside," the country of incorporation); and (3) foreign base-company services income (in general, income from services performed outside the country of incorporation for a related person).[17] A vestige of the unreasonable accumulations, or perhaps more properly the dis-

[16] Statement of Managers on the Part of the House, CCH Standard Federal Tax Reports, Special 13 (Oct. 10, 1962), pp. 18–30.

[17] Throughout the drafting history of the bill, various attempts were made to soften the impact of the measure on investments in less developed countries in order to encourage such investments while discouraging investments in developed countries. As a result, a complicated series of exceptions and qualifications for less developed countries were added. These and other special exceptions will be summarized separately.

guised dividend, approach remains since the shareholders are also required to include pro rata shares of the increase in the foreign corporation's earnings invested in the United States property.

The 1962 act contains three major qualifications designed to exclude from its provisions those controlled foreign subsidiaries which gain little or no tax advantage from third-country operations. These three qualifications are the minimum distributions provision, the 30 percent rule, and the "substantial reduction of taxes" rule.

The most important of these qualifications is the minimum distribution provision. The purpose of this exception is to free shareholders in certain cases from inconvenience and possibly increased taxation resulting from the general tax-haven provisions. Such a purpose would be served when the foreign corporation is not used to secure a combined foreign and domestic tax rate lower than the domestic tax rate faced by a comparable domestic firm investing in the United States. This purpose reflects the general policy of securing equality between U. S. residents doing business abroad and those doing business at home. Under the minimum distribution mechanism, a shareholder may elect not to include in gross income any foreign base-company income where he receives a sufficiently large distribution of the foreign corporation's current earnings and profits. This alternative may be elected if the foreign tax paid plus the U. S. tax on the distribution, less the foreign tax credit, is approximately equal to the tax that would be paid by a domestic corporation with comparable U. S. earnings. A "sliding scale" is set forth in the statute prescribing the minimum distribution of income for given effective foreign tax rates. The scale

Effective foreign tax rate	Required minimum distribution as percentage of earnings and profits
Less than 10	90
10–20	86
20–28	82
28–34	75
34–39	68
39–42	55
42–44	40
44–46	27
46–47	14
47 or over	0

is so constructed that the minimum distribution required is slightly lower than that needed to achieve the equality just described; a slight preference for foreign over domestic income thus remains, even though such foreign income results from tax-haven operations.

The second qualification to the general provisions of the 1962 legislation is the 30 percent rule. This rule treats a controlled foreign corporation as if it had no foreign base-company income whatever, when it constitutes less than 30 percent of gross income. Thus, where foreign base-company income constitutes only a minor portion of total income, the new legislation does not affect U. S. shareholders. Furthermore, to simplify accounting problems at the other end of the scale, all gross income is treated as foreign base-company income where foreign base-company income exceeds 70 percent of gross income.

Finally, on proof satisfactory to the Treasury that the creation of a controlled foreign subsidiary does not substantially reduce taxes on any items of the income of the subsidiary, none of that income has to be treated as foreign base-company income. In the light of the proposed Treasury regulations, this exclusion will probably be available only when the taxes paid on the income in question are not less than 90 percent of the taxes that would have been paid if the subsidiary had been organized in the country of "use, consumption, or destination" in the case of sales income, or the country where the services were performed in the case of services income.

The three foregoing qualifications—the minimum distribution provision, the 30 percent rule, and the "substantial reduction of taxes" provision—may be considered mere concessions to taxpayer convenience rather than major departures from the spirit of the legislation. But two additional exceptions—the export trade corporation exemption and the less developed countries provisions— must be deemed major departures from the anti-tax haven approach.

The Export Trade Corporation provisions create a new class of foreign corporation, the Export Trade Corporation, for which special rules are prescribed. The U. S. shareholder of an American-controlled foreign corporation which constitutes an Export Trade

Corporation need not include in gross income that portion of the foreign corporation's foreign base-company income which constitutes export trade income to the extent that such export trade income is invested in export trade assets. The amount that may be excluded is subject to two special limitations. The maximum amount a U. S. shareholder may exclude is the lesser of one and one-half times export promotion expenses, or 10 percent of gross receipts, allocable to export trade income. The exception is not as broad as it might at first appear to be. Its scope is determined not only by the two special limitations but also by the definitions of the new major concepts—Export Trade Corporation, export trade income, and export trade assets.

An Export Trade Corporation is in general a corporation that derives 90 percent of gross income from sources outside the United States, provided that 75 percent of its gross income constitutes export trade income. This definition limits the benefits of the exception to export operations and will normally require enterprises with foreign manufacturing operations and exports to establish a special foreign export subsidiary to qualify for these benefits. Export trade income is, of course, defined to exclude manufacturing and portfolio investment income; but within those limits it is broadly defined to include profits, commissions, fees, and other compensation from the sale to unrelated persons for "use, consumption, or disposition" outside the United States of property "manufactured, produced, grown or extracted" in the United States, and from services related to such property. Export trade assets are those assets directly related to an export business, including working capital, inventory, physical facilities, and credit to purchasers. This definition, although not illiberal in its conception of assets necessary to an export business, deters the use of export earnings to finance manufacturing or portfolio investment.

The two special limitations may also restrict the benefits of the Export Trade Corporation provisions. The limitation of one and one-half times the export promotion expenses will not be burdensome as long as the export business of an enterprise is in a development stage, since export promotion expenses are defined broadly to include salaries, rentals, depreciation, and other ordinary and necessary expenses related to export trade income. It may, however, be limiting for well-established profitable export operations. The other special limitation, 10 percent of gross receipts allocable to export trade income, will affect the more profitable export subsidiaries.

If one considers that the inclusion of the Export Trade Corporation provisions in the foreign income provisions with the tacit approval of the Treasury is indicative of a coherent policy rather than a bargaining compromise, it provides some interesting insights into the present U. S. policy toward the taxation of foreign income. Tax-haven operations are sanctioned if exports are promoted because the effect is favorable for the U. S. balance of payments. Foreign investments directly related to export businesses are favored because they tend to promote U. S. exports and thus improve the U. S. balance of payments. If profits are used to finance manufacturing or portfolio investments, however, the benefits of the Export Trade Corporation provisions are lost, presumably because the time of repatriating earnings from such investments is thought too remote. Immediate repatriation of the export income is thought preferable to the future repatriation of earnings from investments of the same funds in foreign manufacturing facilities or in foreign securities.

It is now impossible for anyone to determine how important the Export Trade Corporation provisions may be. Their effect will depend on the degree to which circumstances and ingenuity of counsel enable U. S. enterprises to meet the rigorous definitions and limitations. Perhaps the greatest importance of the provisions rests in the principles they establish. The approach is a step in the direction of the United Kingdom's Overseas Trade Corporation, a class of domestic U. K. corporation exempt from U. K. tax on foreign-source income of any nature. Should the pendulum swing back toward the kind of thinking underlying the 1959 Boggs bill, the Export Trade Corporation provisions of the 1962 statute may prove to be the legislative prototype of a greatly broadened foreign business corporation exemption.

The less developed countries provisions, like the Export Trade Corporation provisions, are a major departure from the general thrust of the 1962 legislation. This special treatment is apparently designed to encourage, or at least to avoid discouraging, investment in less developed countries. Dividends, interest, and net gains may be excluded from foreign base-company income if derived from qualified investments in less developed countries but only, in general, if equivalent funds are reinvested in such qualified investments. Qualified investments are defined to include a 10 percent or greater stock interest in a less developed country corporation,[18] certain obligations of a less developed country corporation, and obligations of a less developed country itself. The exception is thus relatively limited; for example, no exemption is created for income from the sale of goods or performance of services.

The 1962 legislation also contains several provisions designed to assure that income deferred by the foreign-source exemption will on repatriation bear the full amount of tax that would have been levied had the deferral privilege not existed. Among such provisions are those dealing with sales or exchanges (including liquidations) of stock in foreign corporations, foreign investment companies, distributions in kind, and transfers of U. S. industrial property rights to foreign corporations.

Under the 1962 act, gains on sales or exchanges (including liquidations) of stock in foreign corporations are to be taxed at ordinary income, rather than capital gains, rates. Such gains are treated as dividends, thus permitting a derivative foreign tax credit on foreign taxes paid by the foreign corporation. While both the House bill and the 1962 Revenue Act as passed denied capital gains treatment to at least a portion of liquidating distributions of foreign corporations, perhaps the most important difference between the two bills was that the House version denied capital gains treatment to such distributions to the extent of all earnings and profits accumulated since February 28, 1913, while in the final

[18] A less developed country corporation is defined as a foreign subsidiary engaged in trade or business in a less developed country, deriving 80 percent or more of its income from less developed countries and with 80 percent or more of its assets located in such countries. Less developed countries are those designated by the President by Executive Order as such. However, the designation must not be applied to the Sino-Soviet bloc and the following countries specified in Internal Revenue Code Sec. 995 (c) (3): Australia, Austria, Belgium, Canada, Denmark, France, Germany (Federal Republic), Hong Kong, Italy, Japan, Liechtenstein, Luxembourg, Monaco, Netherlands, New Zealand, Norway, South Africa, San Marino, Sweden, Switzerland, and United Kingdom. The designation may not be terminated without thirty-day prior notice being given to Congress. Under Executive Order of December 27, 1962, all the countries not prohibited were designated less developed.

version the date was December 31, 1962. To established foreign enterprises, the difference is enormous, since in most cases the initial investment was small and growth has occurred largely through reinvestment.

Distributions of property in kind by foreign corporations must be valued by corporate shareholders at fair market value. The shareholder is no longer permitted to value the property held by the distributing corporation at its adjusted basis. The new rule prevents the shareholder from realizing the appreciation of corporate property at capital gains rates when distributed in kind and then sold as property.

If a U. S. corporation sells to its foreign subsidiary industrial property rights, such as patents and secret processes, the gains it derives are no longer entitled to capital gains treatment but must be reported as ordinary income.

Ordinary income treatment is also required for sales and exchanges of stock in foreign investment companies on earnings and profits accumulated after December 31, 1962, unless the foreign investment company registers as an investment company with the Securities and Exchange Commission and elects to distribute currently at least 90 percent of its ordinary income, and the shareholder reports currently the capital gains of the foreign investment company. Only foreign investment companies with more than 50 percent U. S. ownership are subject to the act, but, unlike the controlled foreign corporation provisions, all U. S. shareholders are counted whether or not they own a 10 percent interest. Capital gains treatment is still permitted, however, where the foreign subsidiary is a less developed country corporation, provided the stock has been owned for a continuous period of ten years before the sale or exchange.

The 1962 legislation also contained a "grossing-up" requirement designed to eliminate the overall effective rate differential favoring repatriated foreign subsidiary income over branch income. The U. S. parent of a foreign corporation is required to include within gross income both the amount of dividends received from its foreign subsidiary and the amount of the foreign taxes paid by the foreign subsidiary (thus "grossing-up" the dividend), but is permitted to credit the full amount of the foreign taxes paid by the subsidiary. The new "grossing-up" requirement for computing the derivative foreign tax credit does not apply if the latter is a less developed country corporation. Thus, the pre-1962 formula for calculating the tax liability on income from investment in less developed countries is still available.

Probable Effects of the 1962 Legislation

The tax-haven provisions are likely to reduce the volume of after-tax foreign income available for remittance or reinvestment, since the ability to avoid foreign taxes is reduced and the effective foreign tax thereby raised. Whether this factor would induce foreign subsidiaries to distribute less to their U. S. shareholders and to maintain the level of reinvestment can only be a matter of conjecture. There probably will be reduction in the incentive to invest and reinvest abroad on the part of those U. S. investors and those U. S. subsidiaries with foreign earnings who consider their returns before distribution. For those investors, however, who consider returns only as distributed dividends, the tax-haven provisions are not likely to make a difference in the incentive to invest abroad. Moreover, since the tax-haven provisions do not apply to foreign corporations which are less than 50 percent U. S. owned, or to investors with less than 10 percent participation, no effect on the incentives of those investors should result.

Some of the results of the grossing-up provisions can be anticipated. They will narrow the tax differential for distributed income earned at home and abroad, since foreign-source income of U. S. corporate shareholders is subject to the full U. S. tax rate or the foreign rate, whichever is higher. Grossing up places the remitted earnings of foreign subsidiaries on the same tax basis as foreign branch earnings, and thus reduces the significance of the difference in form of business organization.

The limitation of grossing-up to the developed countries will provide some incentive both to invest and reinvest in the less developed countries instead of the developed countries. The combination of tax-haven and grossing-up provisions, in their application to income accruing in the developed countries, may encourage the diversion of this income toward reinvestment in the less developed countries (after paying the U. S. tax liability) and a larger repatriation of income from the less developed countries. Although it provides a favorable tax differential to new investments, the continuation of the old method of computing the credit for foreign taxes paid by less developed country corporations will not provide the added incentive to reinvestment of earnings from capital already existing in the less developed countries which grossing up might have given.

The exemption permitting capital gains treatment on sales or exchanges of the stock of less developed country corporations could be significant. In countries where the foreign tax rate is sufficiently low, the ability to accumulate and then repatriate foreign earnings in liquidation at the lower tax rates permitted under capital gains treatment tends to encourage new U. S. investment in the foreign country and relatively short-lived reinvestments of foreign earnings. If the foreign tax rate is higher than the U. S. rate, the above situation does not apply. Since tax rates in underdeveloped countries show wide variations in relation to the United States, the continuation of this tax treatment is not likely to have a significant effect on capital formation in these countries. However, the effect may be important in individual countries that offer tax exemptions to U. S. investors. In such countries, a larger flow of new capital investment may be obtained at the expense of reduced investment periods. However, the introduction of the requirement that the stock be held for ten years prior to sale or liquidation may greatly reduce this undesirable effect.

Tax Regulations Resulting from the 1962 Act

The new legislation has posed many difficult problems in formulating tax regulations. In particular, there are the following:

1. The provisions defining a controlled foreign corporation require tax regulations to attribute control as ownership changes.

2. Applying the minimum distribution provision will be difficult in cases of a chain of subsidiaries and, particularly, where withholding taxes are imposed by the foreign countries and a lower corporate tax rate is placed on distributed earnings.

3. Determining foreign base-company income may require

businesses to keep burdensome records. However, the regulations may alleviate this in the case of firms with little base-company income, by requiring them only to show that the major part of their income is from manufacturing, or that a minimum distribution was made, to avoid wherever possible the need to give accounting for base-company income receipts.

4. The old problems associated with the definition of a controlled foreign corporation, as one in which at least 50 per cent of the voting stock is owned by U. S. stockholders, each with a minimum 10 percent participation, are aggravated under the new legislation because the tax-haven provisions apply to these types of American-controlled corporations. There is also the problem of evading the provisions by manipulating stock ownership.

5. Establishing the U. S. tax liability on foreign-source income according to the U. S. rules when the books of account are kept on a local basis could pose formidable problems. This is particularly true, for example, since earnings and profits are now subject to full taxation on liquidation. The Internal Revenue Service has issued a policy statement that foreign earnings and profits must be estimated according to U. S. rules. In practice, however, there can only be an approximation, with adjustments made in the foreign accounts only where the foreign rules differ greatly from U. S. rules. Investment allowances, special reserves, and evaluation of assets are cases in point.

Revenue Consequences of the 1962 Act

The new legislation is also bound to have some effect on revenue collected by the United States. Estimates of the effects of various proposals are tenuous and, at best, give only an approximation of possible consequences. However, some estimates, discussed below, were developed by the Treasury in connection with the Revenue Act of 1962.

Eliminating the deferral privilege probably would increase the revenues of the United States government for two reasons. First, if reinvested earnings of foreign subsidiaries become part of the permanent capitalization of foreign operations, the earnings will never be repatriated and, with the deferral privilege, the U. S. tax liability will never arise. Second, if foreign earnings are growing over time, postponing the tax liability on those earnings that are eventually repatriated amounts to reducing the stream of taxes being paid to the United States government.

The Treasury estimated that eliminating deferral would yield an immediate increase in tax revenues of $100 million from income currently channeled through so-called tax havens and $80 million from earnings in developed countries for a total of $180 million. Putting restrictions on tax havens, but allowing a continuation of tax deferral as contained in the original version of the tax bill passed by the House of Representatives (H.R. 10650), was estimated to provide an increase in tax receipts of only $85 million from the tax-haven operations. Since the Revenue Act of 1962 as finally passed was even less demanding on tax-haven operations than H.R. 10650, the estimates should be reduced further.

Other aspects of the Revenue Act of 1962 in the foreign-source income field were also expected to yield increases in revenue. The grossing-up provision was estimated to provide $25 million. However, if the grossing-up provision were combined with elimination of tax deferral, it was estimated that tax revenue increases would amount to $90 million. A number of other provisions were estimated to yield from $30 to $60 million.

CHAPTER IV

Economic Effects of Taxing Foreign-Source Income

CONSIDERATIONS INFLUENCING the choice of a system of taxation fall into two categories—tax neutrality and tax equity. Neutrality and equity are related but different concepts. Both are desirable for reaching a status of equality in our tax laws, and the Treasury linked them together as the goals of its recommendations in 1961.[1] Unfortunately, conflicting interpretations of the meaning of the concepts led to widespread confusion in the subsequent congressional hearings. On the one hand, tax neutrality is related to economic decision making and, to achieve it, decisions must be unaffected by the tax laws themselves. Tax equity, on the other hand, is related to the relative burdens of taxes borne by different taxpayers and, to achieve it, equal sacrifices in bearing the tax burdens must be made. These key issues too often are misunderstood. They are, therefore, discussed at length before considering the effects of foreign investment on domestic economic growth and the balance of payments.

Neutrality and Equity

In the issue at hand, tax neutrality is justified for the same rea-

[1] *Revenue Act of 1962*, Hearings before the Senate Committee on Finance, 87 Cong. 2 sess. (1962), Pt. I.

44

sons that freedom of international capital movements is desired. If capital is free to seek the highest rewards possible and no other distortions intervene, returns to all factors of production—including wages, interest, rents, and profits—will increase because total output will be at a maximum. This is as true for capital flows between countries as it is for flows within a country. Stated generally, world welfare will be increased if capital is free to move from countries where the rate of return is low to those where it is high.[2] Welfare will presumably increase through these movements until the expected rates of return, properly discounted for real commercial risk, are equalized around the world. The rates of return in these calculations are derived independently of the existence of a tax system, but in reality, private investment decisions are based on after-tax rates of return. If a tax system distorts the after-tax profitability between two investments, or between two investors, making the relative attractiveness differ from what it would have been had there been no tax, then it is not neutral.[3] If the tax system is not neutral, maximum world welfare will not be achieved, because capital will not be distributed most efficiently. Conversely, a neutral tax would not influence any aspect of the investment decision, such as the location of the investment or the nationalities of the investors.

The neutrality issue may be divided into two parts, domestic and foreign. (1) Domestic neutrality implies equal treatment of Americans investing at home and Americans investing abroad. (2) Foreign neutrality implies equal treatment of Americans investing in foreign operations and their non-American competitors.

To obtain a tax system that theoretically has domestic neutrality, the burden of taxes on profits received from each new dollar of investment must be equalized in all areas. In contrast, to obtain a tax system having foreign neutrality, the total tax burden on American foreign investment must be the same as that on foreign nationals. At first glance, it seems that tax neutrality in both senses would be possible if all tax jurisdictions equalized the rates of all taxes that fall on profits. Even without this, a single taxing authority

[2] To be strictly true, the prices of all goods and factors must equal their marginal costs, and no external economies or diseconomies must exist—that is, all conditions for a Pareto optimum must be satisfied.

[3] The tax system may be neutral but the fiscal system nonneutral if government expenditures discriminate in some way.

could at least aim at domestic neutrality. It could do so by imposing the same tax rate on the profits of all its citizens, regardless of where they earned their income, and by granting a tax credit for profit taxes paid to a foreign taxing authority for foreign-source income. If the foreign tax rate were less than the domestic rate, a domestic tax liability would accrue and would have to be paid on all income at the time it was earned. This means that on foreign-source income, the tax would have to be paid whether or not the income were repatriated as dividends; no deferral privilege would be granted.[4] If the foreign tax rate were more than the domestic rate, the government would have to take one of two courses. It could permit the use of the excess tax credit to pay a tax liability arising from domestic earnings; or it could pay a direct subsidy to offset the excessive tax paid abroad. The theoretical requirements for domestic neutrality, however, provide an ambiguous guideline for tax policy. Many practical considerations modify opinions on domestic neutrality. These must be considered in detail before a judgment can be made on the overall neutrality position of the U. S. laws.

Domestic Neutrality

In presenting the proposed Revenue Act of 1962 to Congress, the Treasury interpreted the prescription for theoretical domestic tax neutrality to mean that the corporate income tax should be immediately levied on the foreign-source income of controlled foreign subsidiaries. The tax would not wait for the repatriation of that income, but the proposal would allow a credit against the U. S. tax liability for corporate income taxes, or their equivalent, paid to a foreign government. It was argued that if deferral were continued for controlled foreign subsidiaries, the taxpayer could use the money representing the potential tax liability until repatriation occurred. He could use it to earn additional income. Therefore, the government would really be providing the equivalent of an interest-free loan amounting to the government claim on earnings that had not been repatriated. Since the option is not available on earnings from domestic investments, this aspect of the tax system favors foreign over domestic investment, and this does not provide domes-

---

[4] For an extensive discussion of the theoretical issues see Peggy B. Richman, *Taxation of Foreign Investment Income* (The Johns Hopkins Press, 1963).

tic neutrality. In addition, however, many factors must be considered to determine whether the marginal tax burden is being equalized at home and abroad or whether such equalization is desirable. These considerations tend to destroy the precise determination of domestic neutrality.

First, the definitions of taxable income, as well as the applicable tax rate, must be uniform. For example, if either domestic or foreign operations are given greater leeway with respect to the accounting of depreciation for tax purposes, or if the definitions of taxable income are not uniform, domestic neutrality may not be achieved. If one source of income allows investment credits not available to the other, or if income from one source is subject to more lenient carry-forward and carry-back provisions than the other, equal statutory tax rates will mean unequal tax burdens, and, therefore, will not be neutral.

Second, domestic neutrality demands that all taxes bearing on profits be equalized. It could be argued that direct taxes, such as the corporate income tax, are not shifted but are borne completely out of profits, and that all indirect taxes are completely shifted forward to the consumer or to other factors of production. Under such an assumption, one must concentrate on equalizing the corporate income tax rate alone. Much research in public finance, however, indicates that such rigid assumptions are not justified. Recent reports of research indicate that, when the entire economy is considered, the incidence of a tax apparently cannot be determined by just looking at the party on whom the tax is levied and at parties dealing with the original taxpayer. Instead, one must look at the total effect of the tax on the whole economy after successive rounds of transactions. A full-scale discussion of tax incidence is beyond the scope of this study, but the issues involved are quite pertinent to our subject. If part of the indirect tax burden does fall on profits, the fact that foreign countries generally levy heavier indirect taxes than the United States cannot be ignored in determining domestic neutrality. The difficulty would also appear if the indirect rates were the same among countries, but the portion shifted was different.

A third area of major concern involves the purposes for which tax receipts are spent. Governments can spend revenues to provide firms in the private sector of the economy with services or goods that they would otherwise have to purchase themselves. Such goods and services must be considered in determining domestic neutrality. If the amount of government benefits provided abroad differed from that provided domestically by the United States government, tax rates must differ to account for these benefits if domestic neutrality is to be achieved. To take an extreme example, if the tax liability of an enterprise were determined solely by the "market value" of necessary services it received from the government (benefit principle of taxation), taxes should be considered like any other cost of production. Under this assumption, neutrality between domestic and foreign investment would demand that the U. S. tax on foreign-source income not exceed the value of services provided by the United States government for the foreign operation, and no credit should be given to the firm for taxes paid to a foreign government. Looking at the proposition more realistically, the major part of a firm's tax liability is determined by the level of pre-tax income it achieves (tax principle of ability to pay) and, in the main, is unrelated to the value of the services it receives from the government. However, the amount of services provided by governments differs substantially from country to country. In order logically to overlook these differences in determining domestic neutrality, one must assume that the direct benefits that firms receive from governmental expenditures in different countries are unrelated to the level of income taxation in those countries. This assumption also seems extreme, since government expenditures and income are related; thus one must consider the substantial differences in services provided by the government in determining domestic neutrality.

A fourth qualification to the prescription for arriving at domestic tax neutrality and its desirability involves the subjective determination of risk. In determining the size of expected rates of return on capital in different countries, how does one arrive at the proper discount for real commercial risk? The expected rate of return on an investment comes from calculating an average value for all possible rates of return, and the estimation of real risk comes from the variance of this theoretical distribution. Obviously, the theoretical distribution of all possible rates of return is not known in advance. For investment planning, the expected rate of return and risk must be determined subjectively, but these determinations may well be biased through either ignorance or prejudice. For example, investment opportunities at home may be better known than foreign ones. Or the potential investor may be suspicious of foreign investment because of an alien language or culture. In such circumstances, he might add a higher risk premium on foreign investment than would be justified—and, thus, he would invest too little abroad. It could be argued, in such an instance, that domestic tax neutrality implies that tax offsets for losses should be more liberal on foreign-source income than on domestic income, or that a nonneutral tax favoring foreign investment is desirable.

A final comment concerning the theoretical implications of domestic tax neutrality should be made. A movement toward neutrality in taxation is a desirable goal only if all other requirements for an optimal world economy already exist. If there are distortions in the market place because of monopoly elements in buying or selling, or because of external economies, or because of governmental influences, or for other reasons, the market prices of goods and factors of production will not properly reflect their true economic value. In such circumstances, the expected rates of return on various investment opportunities will not accurately represent the value to society of capital in alternative uses. From a priori considerations, tax neutrality may not be desired, since an improvement in world welfare will occur if a nonneutral tax compensates for the misallocation of capital encouraged by other distortions in the economy. It is as possible that world welfare considerations will require a movement away from tax neutrality as a movement toward it.[5]

If the foregoing theory is taken literally, it implies that policy recommendations could never be made since theoretical optimum conditions never exist. However, national policy decisions must be made, and those responsible for them must reach conclusions even though there may be no firm theoretical justification for them. Also, a review of policy decisions is useful and necessary despite the lack of theoretical certainty. If it is recognized that differential taxes could affect the business decision on the location of investment and could affect its success, neutrality must be determined, even though the method used may be crude by theoretical standards and based mainly on judgment rather than fact.

[5] R. K. Lancaster and R. G. Lipsey, "The General Theory of Second Best," *The Review of Economic Studies*, Vol. 24 (1956–57), pp. 11–32.

This raises the question of the degree to which the actual tax practice in the United States coincides with the theoretical norm. The United States taxes foreign-earned income at the same corporate income tax rate as domestically earned income, and it allows a tax credit for income taxes (or their equivalent) paid to foreign governments, as domestic neutrality requires. Nevertheless, at least four aspects of U. S. tax law depart from theoretical neutrality. First, no investment tax credit is allowed on foreign investment as it is on domestic investment, and the rules for carrying income and losses backward and forward are less liberal on foreign operations. Second, the tax credit that can be claimed for taxes paid to a foreign government is limited by the U. S. law to the amount of tax liability that would have been due had the income been earned in the United States. If foreign income tax rates are greater than U. S. rates, this limitation is important. Third, the U. S. tax laws provide special tax rules for foreign investment in the Western Hemisphere if the operation qualifies and is organized as a Western Hemisphere Trading Corporation (WHTC).[6] The favorable tax situation that these rules allow is not only a departure from domestic tax neutrality; it also violates the general U. S. policy of not discriminating among countries in foreign economic matters. Fourth, the United States defers its tax claim on incomes earned by foreign subsidiaries until they are repatriated as dividends to their parent corporations. This apparent departure from domestic neutrality is important only if effective foreign tax rates are below those of the United States (the converse of item two above). Table 2 lists the maximum corporate income tax rates for a selected group of countries. While some less developed countries provide substantially lower tax rates, industrially advanced countries appear to have statutory corporate income tax rates roughly in line with those of the United States although effective rates may well be lower.

The existence of tax deferral, as discussed earlier, was the main focal point of controversy during the tax hearings on the Revenue Act of 1962. And the Treasury officials recommended that it be ended because they believed it violates the canons of domestic neutrality. In opposing the Treasury position, it was argued that the deferral privilege promotes neutrality since foreign subsidiaries do

[6] See earlier discussion of the WHTC and other special rules in Chap. 1.

TABLE 2. Maximum Corporate Statutory Income Tax Rates in
Selected Countries

Country	Rate (Percent)
Argentina	42
Australia	40
Belgium	28.5[a]
Brazil	30
Canada	50
Chile	25
Colombia	45
France	50
West Germany	51[b]
Italy	31[c]
Japan	49[d]
Mexico	52
Netherlands	47
United Kingdom	53.5
United States	48[e]
Venezuela	40

Source: U. S. Treasury: in part presented in Exhibit III, *Revenue Act of 1962*, Hearings before the Senate Committee on Finance, 87 Cong. 2 sess. (1962), Pt. 1.

[a] Income tax paid in the previous year is deductible so that the nominal rate of 40 percent is reduced to approximately 28.5 percent.

[b] The German corporate rate of 51 percent is reduced to approximately 22 percent if all profits are distributed.

[c] This rate is increased by 15 percent on profits in excess of 6 percent of capital plus certain allowable reserves.

[d] The rate on distributed profits is 42 percent.

[e] Post transition rate under the Revenue Act of 1964.

not have the same benefits available to domestic corporations (and foreign branches), such as loss carry-over, depletion, etc.; because they are not allowed a tax credit for indirect taxes borne out of profits; and, in general, because deferral is necessary to counteract other inequities.

Judging the seriousness of tax deferral and other breaches of domestic neutrality is difficult. Unequal treatment of the investment tax credit and the like puts foreign investment in a position somewhat less favorable than domestic investment. This breach of neutrality can be defended by saying that a more important public policy goal, the stimulation of domestic economic growth, is being served. The limitation of the tax credit for income taxes paid foreign governments may be insignificant. Only the United Kingdom has rates markedly above the United States (Table 2), and the ability of firms through the "over-all limitation" to pool all foreign income may be sufficient to cover an isolated case. If the United States reduced its corporate income tax rate while other developed countries did not, this departure from neutrality would become more important, as a number of countries now have statutory tax rates very close to that of the United States. This departure may also be justified, since the United States cannot permit a complete tax credit without an upper limit for fear of having a significant erosion of its domestic tax base through actions of foreign governments. The departure from neutrality resulting from Western Hemisphere Trading Corporations may also be defended because it helps achieve another public policy goal. The stimulation of private investment in certain underdeveloped countries and of U. S. exports, resulting from the WHTC legislation, may be desirable.

As to the deferral privilege, Table 2 indicates a number of rates substantially below the 48 percent U. S. rate. Therefore, this departure from domestic neutrality could be very important, particularly for the less developed countries and a few others. It could be even more important if the effective tax rates on income earned in developed countries differed substantially from the maximum rates listed in Table 2. Allowing generous deductions against taxable income is one method by which a reduction of effective tax rates is accomplished. Another method, the use of so-called tax-haven corporations, may provide a very large reduction. However, the treatment of the tax-haven problem, as discussed earlier, in the Revenue Act of 1962 may have ended this form of abuse.

The tax deferral privilege may also be justified on a number of grounds previously discussed. It may be needed to offset the burden placed on profits in foreign countries by having a higher level of indirect taxation. It may compensate, in part, for a difference in services provided by the government for business firms. Finally, it may be necessary to encourage those who overestimate the risk in foreign investment. At best, one can say that, given the deferral privilege, no unqualified judgment can be given on domestic neutrality. If foreign rates are close to the U. S. rate, it is not clear whether the removal of the deferral privilege would increase or decrease tax neutrality. If, however, the rates differ greatly, it is unlikely that the factors could compensate for the advantage that deferral gives foreign investment.

Foreign Neutrality

The problems in appraising the foreign neutrality of U. S. taxation of foreign-source income differ substantially from those involved in assessing domestic neutrality. Theoretically, foreign neutrality could be obtained if the tax burden placed on the foreign subsidiaries of U. S. firms were the same as that placed on the foreign-owned competitors of U. S. subsidiaries operating in the same countries. Many businessmen have criticized the Treasury for failing to give sufficient attention to foreign neutrality. It was argued that if U. S. foreign subsidiaries have to carry a heavier tax burden than their foreign competitors, the rate of growth of the U. S. firms will be hindered, they will lose ground in the competitive race, and both American firms and the U. S. balance of payments will ultimately suffer.

As a practical matter, there are really two types of competitors that subsidiaries of U. S. corporations meet in their foreign operations: firms owned by residents of the country in which the operation takes place, and firms operated as the foreign subsidiaries of residents of countries other than the United States. If foreign countries also tax the subsidiaries of their domestic firms operating in other countries, there may be various levels of taxes being borne by competitors within the same tax jurisdiction. Since all firms must pay the taxes levied by the country of operation, those owned by nationals of the country of operation will bear the lowest level of taxation. If the United States wished to equalize the tax burden placed on American-controlled foreign subsidiaries with locally owned firms, it must forsake the nationality principle of taxation and forego all taxes on foreign operations. While this may bring foreign neutrality with one group of competitors, it certainly would not be domestically neutral. If the United States wanted to equalize the tax burden of American-controlled foreign subsidiaries with other foreign subsidiaries in the country of operations, it would have to gear the U. S. tax system to that of several other countries. Such action is neither feasible nor desirable. More basically, taxation of foreign-source income involves the problem of overlapping tax jurisdictions, which by itself will always prevent the realization of foreign neutrality (except for the one case when all countries equalize their tax rates on all types of levies). Because achieving foreign tax neutrality is impossible in different situations it cannot be the principal guide for tax policy.

The Equity Issue

An equitable tax, as already noted, will impose substantially the same tax burden on all citizens who are similarly situated and who are located in the same tax jurisdiction. The desirability of equity rests on the belief that all taxpayers should bear their proper share of the burdens of operating the government—or simply on the moral ground of fairness. There also is a practical side of the equity issue, for an equitable tax will encourage voluntary compliance (and vice versa), on which a great deal of U. S. taxation is dependent. Taxing foreign-source income presents a second question, whether the international tax base is equitably divided among countries. This second question has some historical interest, but was not discussed during recent U. S. tax debates. Furthermore, because it is not amenable to the tax policy of any single country, it will not be discussed here.[7]

A dispute over the equity issue arose when the general prescription for equity was applied to the case of foreign-source income taxation. The Treasury argued that since the United States uses the nationality principle in claiming tax jurisdiction, American-owned foreign investment is in the same tax jurisdiction as domestic investment and a dollar earned by an American should be taxed equally, regardless of where it is earned; and, specifically, that tax deferral should be ended. Opponents of the Treasury's view argued that equity can only be achieved if American-owned foreign investment is forced to bear the same tax burden as the foreign competitors that they meet on foreign soil (the same as foreign neutrality). Their argument, therefore, was that the only relevant tax jurisdiction is the national entity in which income is earned, and that the situation of American-owned foreign subsidiaries is similar to that of foreign-owned firms operating in the country in question.

On the one hand, the Treasury's definition of equity certainly is open to question. Even if American-owned foreign subsidiaries are

[7] For a discussion, see Richman, *op. cit.*

in the same tax jurisdiction as domestic firms, they cannot be described as similarly situated. Many of the arguments against domestic neutrality also apply here. Foreign subsidiaries are subject to taxes imposed by the country in which they are located and they may not be completely reimbursed by the U. S. tax credit. Furthermore, foreign subsidiaries do not necessarily benefit from expenditures of the United States government as much as domestic operations. If the two taxpayers are not similarly situated, there is no basis for determining tax equity. On the other hand, the opponents of the Treasury's view present an equally unconvincing case for their concept of equity. Even accepting their restricted definition of taxing jurisdiction, it is still difficult to argue that American-owned subsidiaries and their foreign competitors are similarly situated. Foreign subsidiaries of U. S. corporations have access to the largest and cheapest capital market in the world because of their attachment to an American owner. Furthermore, the U. S. subsidiaries share in the advanced technology of the United States which, in part, reflects the publicly supported educational system here (not to mention the United States government's direct subsidies to research). American-owned subsidiaries have other advantages that are either unavailable to their foreign competitors or accessible only at greatly enhanced prices. The competitors are thus not similarly situated.

Neither the Treasury's concept of equity nor that of its critics can be accepted as a guide for the taxation of foreign-source income by the United States. Since taxing foreign-source income involves the problem of overlapping tax jurisdiction, the only problem of equity subject to policy arises among taxpayers in the same overlapping tax jurisdiction—that is, among American-owned foreign subsidiaries operating in the same foreign country. In this small group, tax equity appears to exist.

Aside from equity-neutrality questions, the elimination of tax deferral on unrepatriated foreign-source income may be desirable itself.[8] The deferral provision is valuable to firms having operations abroad, and its elimination would reduce some of the attraction of foreign investment. If foreign investment is detrimental to domestic

---

[8] The following discussion of this possibility also applies to suggestions for penalties on foreign investment through additional taxation.

economic growth, or causes difficulties for the U. S. balance of payments, policy measures may be needed to reduce such investment. These possibilities will now be investigated.

Domestic Economic Growth

Many would like to tighten the tax rules on foreign investment because they feel foreign investment reduces the level of domestic investment, and thereby inhibits the growth of domestic output.[9] The argument in its simplest form states that if a firm decides to invest in productive facilities abroad, it will be less willing to expand its facilities at home, and will have less funds available for domestic investment. According to this view, the contraction of domestic investment, when combined with the negative multiplier effects within the economy, is bound to exceed any expansionary effects that might accrue from an increase of exports resulting from the foreign investment. This determination includes the positive multiplier effects of such exports, if the increase of exports is less than the increase in foreign investment. Therefore, foreign investment would lead to a slower growth of domestic output.

This argument needs to be examined in detail to determine under what conditions and to what extent it may be valid. There is an important distinction between the financial transfer involved in a foreign investment and the real transfer of resources to foreigners resulting from the investment. Furthermore, it is important to consider the degree to which domestic resources are used. For this economic problem, as for many others, the existence of unemployment changes the results quite appreciably.

Effect of Foreign Investment with Full Employment

We first assume that demand in the United States is sufficient to use all domestic resources.[10] Foreign investment gives a financial

[9] At this point, it might be useful to distinguish between "national product" and "domestic product." The former encompasses all income of nationally owned factors, including net foreign-source income. The latter includes only income arising within the national boundaries.

[10] The Treasury made this assumption in its presentation in the Hearings before the Senate Finance Committee, *op. cit.*, Pt. 1, pp. 100 and 192.

claim to a foreign entity on U. S. resources. When this financial claim is translated into demand for real resources from the U. S. economy, the amount of resources remaining for domestic uses is correspondingly reduced during the period in which the claim is being exercised. Presenting this idea in symbolic form, the domestic product of the United States is represented by the sum of domestic consumption, domestic investment, government consumption, and exports minus imports:

$$Y = C + I + G + X - M$$

where Y is the real value of domestic product,

C is the real value of domestic consumption,

I is the real value of domestic investment,

G is the real value of government absorption of real output,

X is the real value of exports of goods and services

M is the real value of imports of goods and services.

Making a real transfer of resources abroad involves exporting more goods and services than are currently imported ($X - M$ becomes positive). Since by assumption the domestic product (Y) cannot be increased, the shift in the foreign balance can only result from reducing domestic consumption (C), domestic investment (I), or government consumption (G), or some combination thereof.[11] Assuming that total liquidity within the economy is not excessive (no inflationary pressures), there is a presumption that domestic investment (I) will bear the brunt of the pressure to make the export surplus available. This is so because the financial resources involved in the foreign investment are raised within business firms. Unless these financial resources within firms are replenished, less money will be available for domestic investment in this period. The burden can be shifted in part to consumption, if firms reduce their dividend disbursements to stockholders. This does not seem likely, since dividend expectations are determined by profit levels rather than by the availability of liquid funds—and firms do not like to disappoint stockholders. Firms could seek additional funds from the banking

[11] The difficulties involved in making the real transfer equal the financial transfer are discussed with the balance of payments in the next section. Here, we assume that equilibrium is maintained in the basic balance of payments.

system or directly from the public via flotations of equity or debt securities. Success in these efforts would be in part at the expense of consumption (or conceivably government), but neither alternative seems a very promising source of funds. Monetary policy is likely to be restrictive at times of full employment, making borrowing difficult, and the cost of inducing additional savings from the public may be very great and, therefore, unattractive to business.[12] Thus, domestic investment probably would contract to provide most of the needed export surplus.

A reduction in domestic investment would cause the loss of a future stream of output that would have been produced by the foregone investment (equal to the reduction of investment multiplied by the marginal output-capital ratio). The stream of foregone output would have been distributed in subsequent years among consumption, government, and investment. In such circumstances, future levels of investment would be lower because the real level of domestic product is lower. Future investment may also be lower because the government may need to recover its foregone revenue by taking a larger share of the smaller domestic product. And this, in part, would be at the expense of investment.

There are two types of forces which may offset the factors restricting growth described above. Relative factor prices within the economy will adjust to the lower level of the capital stock (lower than it would have been if domestic investment were higher), and in part will compensate for the change. Since the amount of capital in the economy will be less while the amount of labor will be the same, the demand for labor relative to its supply will be reduced. This implies a shift in factor returns away from wages and toward profits on domestic investment. This shift probably will mean a proportionately higher level of savings and investment in the lower domestic product than would have occurred without it. The opposite will take place in the foreign area receiving the investment, making further investment in those areas less attractive.

The second, and more important, offset to the growth-inhibiting tendencies of foreign investment results from the profits earned by

[12] Firms may well try to borrow abroad to obtain needed funds for foreign investment. Foreign operations are generally a necessary condition for U. S. firms to borrow abroad. While in practice this is important, we are considering as foreign investment, for current purposes, only the net equity in foreign operations provided by Americans.

Americans on their foreign investments. As profits are earned on foreign operations, Americans receive a series of claims over time on output abroad. If earnings are repatriated, the U. S. national income is increased, and the United States can import more goods and services than it pays for through exports out of current domestic production—that is, the foreign balance $(X-M)$ could become negative. This in turn would allow a greater absorption of resources within the economy than are currently being produced, which could lead to larger consumption, government expenditures, and domestic investment. Since these claims are being generated within business firms, the presumption is that a large share could be devoted to domestic investment.

The question of the extent to which the factors inhibiting growth can be offset by other forces depends on: (1) the productivity of the investment foregone in the United States (marginal output-capital ratio) and the distribution of the sacrifice between consumption, government, and investment; and (2) the after-tax profit rate on new foreign investment and the extent to which foreign earnings are repatriated. To completely offset the factors that inhibit growth, the amount of repatriated income from earnings on foreign investment must be great enough to compensate for both the loss of profit on the domestic investment foregone and for the loss of government revenue. Presumably, the rate of profit on foreign investment, after accounting for all taxes that bear on profits, must be greater than the after-tax profit rate on alternative domestic investment, or the enterprise would not have had the incentive to make the foreign investment originally. But the difference is unlikely to be great enough to allow a full offset.

For the national welfare to be served, as distinct from that of the investing enterprise, the after-tax profit rate on the foreign investment should be greater than the pre-tax profit rate on alternative domestic investments. World welfare, however, would appear to be increased if only the pre-tax profit rate on the foreign investment exceeded the pre-tax rate on alternative domestic investments. As for the rate of repatriation of profits, if the differential in profit rates to enterprises is substantial between areas, the incentive will be great to reinvest earnings abroad and repatriate very little, even without tax advantages. Furthermore, if such a differential exists, the incentive for further new foreign investment will exist. This will make the offsetting of the growth-retarding effects of the original investment more difficult. Of course, the transfer of capital abroad will tend to narrow the difference between the expected profit rates on new investment at home and abroad, but the incentive for the foreign investment will not cease until the differential is eliminated (always taking risk differentials into account).

Under conditions of full employment, therefore, it is likely that foreign investment will lead to a lower rate of domestic growth. This sacrifice may be justified if a poor area is being stimulated at the expense of a rich area. Indeed, the history of Western civilization is full of such transfers. In spite of their effect on domestic growth, these transfers may still be desirable, but they must be defended on other grounds.

Effect of Foreign Investment with Unused Resources

Foreign investment will affect domestic growth differently if domestic resources are not fully used. When the financial transfer involved in a foreign investment is converted into demand for real resources in the United States, this need not force a reduction in either consumption, government, or domestic investment, but can be provided from idle capacity. Since domestic investment will not be squeezed through a shortage of resources, domestic growth may not be affected adversely. In fact, the increase in export sales of domestic goods and services that accompanies foreign investment will raise domestic output and, through the positive multiplier process, give a lift to the economy in general. Liquidity pressures might still weigh on the firms making foreign investments. However, with unused capacity in the economy, domestic firms may have been excessively liquid before the foreign transfer or they could recoup their liquidity via the banking system.[13] Subsequent repatriation of earnings might also contribute to domestic growth, since the improved overall profitability of firms might overcome a previous reluctance to invest in domestic ventures. Of course, foreign investment is not the only way of using excess domestic capacity and possibly not the best one.

---

[13] This presumes that the government is following a monetary policy appropriate to the state of the economy.

While domestic growth need not be sacrificed if there are idle resources within the economy, growth could still be retarded by foreign investment. This possibility arises when there is no surplus supply of the specific resources needed to make the real transfer abroad and a bottleneck situation is created. To evaluate this possibility, it is necessary to look at the distribution of resources involved in the transfer from domestic to foreign uses. The transfer would be made in the following categories of goods and services: capital equipment needed for the new venture; raw materials, semi-manufactured goods, and finished manufactured components needed in the production process; management services provided by the firm investing or by consulting firms; services of special knowledge owned by the firm contained in patents and copyrights; and general exports to match expenditures of dollars on locally produced resources.

Each of these categories could become a bottleneck except for special knowledge, which is not exhausted with use. Bottleneck problems are likely to occur, however, only for capital equipment and management services. If the engineering industries of the country are fully employed while there is excess capacity elsewhere in the economy, a transfer of capital equipment abroad probably would cause reduced domestic investment and retarded domestic growth, similar to the full employment case. The loss here would not be as great as under full employment, since resources are available for reallocation from other domestic industries to the bottleneck industry. But such reallocation would require time. Also, if there were a shortage of entrepreneurial or managerial talent, foreign investment could cause less domestic growth. The shortage of trained people needed to perform the functions of organization and decision making may well inhibit growth—and often does in underdeveloped countries. Trained management may also be scarce in a developed country, even when capacity is not fully used, since managerial requirements are not closely related to output levels. This bottleneck can be overcome by relative changes in factor rewards, but the process may be very slow because it rests mainly on the educational system.

In an effort to isolate the effects of foreign investment on domestic economic growth, we have assumed that no balance-of-payments problems result from the investment—that is, the transfer of real resources equals the financial transfer. Under this assumption, we conclude that foreign investment will inhibit domestic growth by diverting resources to foreign uses when there is full employment at home or when a resources bottleneck develops. If the resources required to make the transfer abroad are not being used in the domestic economy, foreign investment may not deter domestic growth; it may encourage it.

The growth-inhibiting conclusion arises from the transfer of real resources from domestic to foreign uses. If the real transfer does not occur, domestic growth will not be deterred directly, but a balance-of-payments problem will be created. In this sense, the reduced domestic growth and balance-of-payments problems can be the alternative consequences of foreign investment. The more the real sources are transferred, the more likely will domestic growth be deterred, but the smaller will be the balance-of-payments problem. Likewise, the less real resources are transferred, the less likely will domestic growth be inhibited, but the larger will be the balance-of-payments problem.

Indirect consequences, however, may permit the domestic growth and the balance-of-payments problems to coexist, and possibly aggravate each other. If facilities abroad arising from U. S. foreign investment produce goods that are sold at the expense of domestic output, foreign investment may cause both problems during a period of insufficient final demand. This possibility will be examined in the next section. Furthermore, if a balance-of-payments problem leads to restrictive monetary and fiscal policies by the government, domestic growth may be sacrificed indirectly even if unnecessarily.

The Balance of Payments[14]

A balance-of-payments problem may result from making a foreign investment if, through the normal operation of market

[14] This section represents an elaboration of previous work by one of the authors in connection with the study by Walter S. Salant and others, *The United States Balance of Payments in 1968* (Brookings Institution, 1963). See, especially, the discussion of direct investment, pp. 139–49.

forces, the real transfer of resources abroad does not equal the financial transfer. The immediate consequence of not covering the financial transfer with real resources will be the accumulation of liquid dollar claims in the hands of foreigners. This increase in liquid dollar liabilities abroad becomes a potential claim against the United States gold stock. The claim would lead to an outflow of gold if these dollar liabilities were not desired by private individuals abroad or foreign governments as portfolio assets, or if the United States could not satisfy the liability in some other way (International Monetary Fund drawings, for instance).

The real burden to the economy of not being able to cover the financial transfer would result from the policies required to bring the balance of payments back into equilibrium. If an internal adjustment were made through restrictive monetary and fiscal policies, the real burden may be the foregone domestic income, if any, and the decline in export prices (so-called terms-of-trade effect). An alternative adjustment through the exchange rate would also imply a deterioration of export prices in relation to import prices if the devaluation were successful, but would be unlikely to reduce the level of domestic activity.[15]

Motives for Foreign Investment

The likelihood of the real transfer being made without difficulty is affected by the characteristics of the country receiving the investment and the nature of the investment itself. The nature of the investment stems from the motivation that encouraged it originally. In general, foreign investment is undertaken because it provides greater prospects for making profits than alternative actions. However, the factors contributing to this expectation vary substantially in individual cases. Investment to develop natural resources will obviously be concentrated in the countries having the resources to develop. Americans may participate in such ventures because they need raw material in their own operations, or because they control a substantial distribution and marketing organization for the resource. Much of the investment of American entrepreneurs in other

---

[15] Other detrimental consequences might also follow currency devaluation, but an analysis of all consequences is beyond the scope of this study.

Western Hemisphere countries has been for this purpose. Another reason for investing abroad is that production costs may be lower than in the United States because of favorable wage rates, raw material prices, or interest rates. Other costs may also be reduced through foreign operations because of the opportunity to reduce transportation costs, distribution costs, inventory and servicing costs to the markets for which the outputs are intended. Foreign production may also be desirable to avoid paying tariffs or to surmount other trade restrictions. Moreover, customers in the country of operations may more readily accept the product if it is manufactured locally. In addition to these factors, the tax laws themselves have a bearing on the foreign investment decision.

TABLE 3. Geographical and Industrial Distribution of the Book Value of U. S. Private Direct Investment, 1962

Item	Total	Canada	Europe	Latin America	Rest of World
Value (Billion dollars)ᵃ	37.1	12.1	8.8	8.5	7.7
Percentage					
Manufacturing	35.6	14.4	13.0	5.1	3.1
Petroleum	34.1ᵇ	7.6	6.4	8.5	11.6
Mining and smelting	8.6	4.0	0.1	3.0	1.5
Public utilities	5.5	1.4	0.1	1.9	2.1
Trade	8.1	1.9	2.9	2.2	1.1
Other industries	8.1ᶜ	3.4	1.3	2.1	1.3
Total	100.0	32.7	23.8	22.8	20.7

Source: Survey of Current Business, Vol. 43 (August 1963).
ᵃ Book value end of year.
ᵇ The 34.1 percent is roughly estimated to be divided as follows: 20 percent, petroleum refining; 14.1 percent, crude petroleum.
ᶜ The 8.1 percent is roughly estimated as 3 percent, agriculture; 5.1 percent, other.

Table 3 provides a clue to the historical importance of some of these motivations. At the end of 1962, the total value of U. S. direct investments abroad amounted to $37.1 billion in contrast to $11.8 billion in 1950. An estimated 28 percent of the total was invested in natural resources (mining and smelting and crude petroleum) and in public utilities. The investment in trade necessary to maintain exports from the United States amounted to 8 percent. The "other industries" category (8.1 percent) includes investments in agriculture and various services such as finance and contracting.

The remaining large segments of investment are in petroleum refining, estimated at 20 percent, and manufacturing at 36 percent. The primary advantage of investing in foreign petroleum refineries comes from the reduction in transportation, distribution, and servicing costs. There is also a saving on tariffs. Political pressures may be exerted to induce companies to set up local refining facilities. As to investment in manufacturing, all of the motives mentioned above are important. As shown in Table 4, direct

TABLE 4. U. S. Private Direct Investment Abroad, by Region and Type of Investment, 1952–56 and 1957–61

(Millions of dollars)

	1952–56[a]				1957–61[a]			
	Canada	Europe	Latin America	Rest of World	Canada	Europe	Latin America	Rest of World
Manufacturing	71	29	35	7	110	255	85	35
Petroleum	184	86	101	117	167	197	231	159
Mining	79	—	63	19	94	—	49	26
Other	73	24	59	30	92	63	42	48
Total	407	139	258	173	463	515	407	268

Sources: 1952–56, U. S. Department of Commerce, *Balance of Payments, Statistical Supplement* (1958); 1957–59, U. S. Department of Commerce, *U. S. Business Investment in Foreign Countries* (1960); 1960–61 latest published data available from *Survey of Current Business.* Philip Bell, *Factors Affecting the United States Balance of Payments,* "Private Capital Movements and the U. S. Balance of Payments Position," Joint Economic Committee, 87 Cong. 2 sess. (1962), Pt. 6.
ᵃ Annual Averages.

investment has recently gone increasingly into petroleum and manufacturing.

Looking at manufacturing investment alone, Europe and Canada together account for most of the total. Although Canada is still the larger of the two, Europe is gaining rapidly. Because of the depression of the thirties and World War II, investment increased in Canada and Latin America from 1929 to 1950 more than in Europe. Since 1950, and especially since 1956, Europe, with its rapid economic growth, has once again attracted U. S. investors.

The formation of the European Economic Community (EEC) and the European Free Trade Association (EFTA) has also attracted U. S. investment to Europe in the last few years. Since exports to EEC (and EFTA) must pay a tariff, while products made within the Common Market can move anywhere inside the tariff wall without paying a duty, U. S. producers are encouraged to invest in manufacturing facilities inside the tariff barrier. And the expanded size of the EEC market encourages the construction of facilities large enough to capture economies of scale. In addition, the risks of a change in tariffs or in other restrictive measures are avoided.

Although it was always possible to surmount a single national tariff wall by direct foreign investment, the EEC arrangement allows entry into four former tariff areas (counting Benelux as a single area) with a single investment. Furthermore, the preferences granted by the Associated Overseas Countries to products made in the member countries of the EEC means that manufacturing facilities within the Common Market provide a cost-saving base for exports to Africa. This produces another incentive for direct investment in the EEC. Getting behind the tariff wall is only one of many reasons for investing in Europe, but it may be the most important one. It is certain, however, that the inducement is directly related to the height of the tariff. As the EEC external tariffs are reduced, there is less incentive to avoid them.

Impact of Direct Investment

It is impossible to determine, and difficult even to estimate, the full impact of direct investment on the balance of payments. To do so the actual values of exports and imports of goods and services must be compared with those that would have occurred in the absence of the investment, as well as the capital movements themselves. We can attempt to analyze the problem, however, and make some empirical estimates to the extent that the limited data allow. These estimates, however, should not obscure the amount of ignorance that abounds in this field. Little is known about why the "typical" business invests abroad and the consequences thereof, or how a change in the tax laws would affect its behavior. For analytical purposes, three stages of effects can be distinguished: the original outflow, the immediate results, and the earnings effect.

The original investment is the value of the financial transfer that must be covered; therefore, it is a negative item in the balance of payments. The stimulus for the real transfer of resources abroad begins almost immediately. The foreign subsidiaries of U. S. firms usually buy a substantial portion of the capital equipment they need from American suppliers, thereby increasing U. S. exports, particularly for investments outside of Europe. Thus, part of the capital outflow may never leave the United States in dollars, but leaves as exports directly linking the financial and real transfers.

Once the foreign facility starts operations, exports from the United States may be increased in several ways. The company may obtain a substantial portion of its raw materials or component parts in the United States. It may buy services from the United States, such as patent rights (royalty fees), management services, technical and engineering services, and the like. The products of a U. S. parent company that are not produced abroad may sell better in foreign countries because the company has better production, distribution, and service facilities abroad. Also, the foreign country's national income may grow from the greater investment, and part of the increased income could be spent buying imports from the United States.

Further consequences flow from the sale of the output from the foreign facility. If natural resources are involved, the output of the raw material might well be sold in the United States (often to the parent firm). Although some of these raw materials compete with domestic output, they mainly make up a deficiency in the U. S. resources endowment. This may lower the net costs of imports substantially. However, if the investment goes into a manufacturing facility that possibly could have been built at home, imports into the United States from the foreign facility might replace domestic production, thereby increasing total U. S. imports. Even if the manufactured products are sold abroad, they may replace the sales of American firms using domestic U. S. facilities; then U. S. exports are reduced.

Determining whether foreign direct investment improves or weakens the U. S. balance of payments may well depend on the extent to which imports displace American production and U. S. exports are displaced by sales from foreign facilities. There is no assurance that a product made by an American firm abroad could have been exported from the United States without foreign investment. If producing in foreign countries yields considerable savings in wages and costs of raw materials, transport, servicing, and distributing, or if the country's tariff barrier is substantial, a foreign firm could make the investment and win the market—if a U. S. firm did not do so. The foreign firm does not even have to be as efficient as the American firm, since the cost differences between the two production sites might be enough to give the foreign producer an edge over products made in the United States.

The situation changes in cases where the American firm produces a unique product, such as a new drug developed through its own research for which its monopoly position is protected by patent laws. Then it is fairly certain that a foreign firm could not take away U. S. sales. The American firm might have a choice of exporting or producing abroad, although foreign governments can influence this decision. Some observers argue that possibly the most unfortunate aspect of foreign investment is the export of the fruits of U. S. research in the form of investments instead of products. However, research is conducted abroad as well as at home. If there is an established market for a product, foreign research efforts will be directed toward finding an alternative product to serve the need for the product. In the long run, the choice between exporting or investing abroad may be illusory, since the export market may be lost to some other producer.

The significance of the export loss probably depends on the area of choice open to businessmen and the likelihood of their having a preference for producing abroad over producing at home and exporting. Businessmen argue that they prefer to produce at home. Foreign operations involve greater risks and entail more management difficulties. Foreign investments are undertaken because costs are less when production facilities are close to marketing centers. As soon as a market reaches the size necessary to capture economies of scale, local production abroad tends to replace U. S. exports. Firms that establish themselves earliest achieve a competitive edge that is hard to overcome. Businessmen also argue that, if the United States is to hold its place in the world economy, American firms must make foreign investments and do so when the market is ripe. Once foreign operations are begun, however, commercial considerations will determine the site of production.

Finally, the balance-of-payments impact of direct investment is related to the earnings from the foreign operations. The balance of payments is improved by any earnings repatriated as income to the U. S. parent firm. While earnings largely depend on business conditions abroad, repatriation depends on the need for funds to finance further investments. Repatriated earnings have been increasing rapidly in recent years both absolutely, as shown in Table 5, and in relation to book value of outstanding foreign investment.

The importance of the various factors affecting the balance of

TABLE 5. U. S. Private Direct Investment Income[a]

(Millions of dollars)

Years	Income from Europe	Income from Rest of World	Total
1950–55, average	157	1,390	1,547
1956	300	1,871	2,171
1957	271	1,978	2,249
1958	291	1,830	2,121
1959	435	1,793	2,228
1960	388	1,967	2,355
1961	478	2,289	2,767
1962	520	2,530	3,050
1963	504	2,568	3,072

Sources: *Survey of Current Business*, Vol. 44 (June 1964), Vol. 43 (March 1963), Vol. 42 (June 1962), Vol. 41 (June 1961), and Vol. 40 (June 1960); U. S. Department of Commerce, *Balance of Payments, Statistical Supplements* (1945–56).

[a] The distribution of earnings between Europe and the rest of the world is tenuous, as some earnings attributed to non-European areas reflect export sales to Europe. The figures include branch profits and income repatriation by subsidiaries.

payments lies in their quantitative significance for the different types of investment in different regions. Since some factors by their nature cannot be observed, and data on others are not available, empirical investigation is difficult. Not only are the important variables not fully discernible, but their reaction to a tax change is completely unknown. Since there were no general changes in the laws governing the taxation of foreign-source income before 1962, there was no reaction to evaluate. However, some judgments can be made.

Table 6 shows estimates for the relevant factors for which some data can be found. Only in the case of manufacturing are there

TABLE 6. Basic Parameter Values for Measuring the Effect of Direct Foreign Investment on the U. S. Balance-of-Payments Position[a]

Item	1957–60		1957	1959–60
	r	a	f	x
Manufacturing investment				
Canada	0.096	0.423	0.018	0.177
Europe	.168	.518[b]	.025	.041
Latin America	.090	.302	.016	.415
Rest of World	.187	.451	.024	.478
Petroleum investment				
Canada	.040	.428	n.a.	n.a.
Europe	.090	.748	n.a.	n.a.
Latin America	.158	.401	n.a.	n.a.
Rest of World	.246	.611	n.a.	n.a.
All industries				
Canada	.074	.416	n.a.	n.a.
Europe	.148	.506	n.a.	n.a.
Latin America	.112	.335	n.a.	n.a.
Rest of World	.202	.462	n.a.	n.a.

Source: Philip Bell, "Private Capital Movements and the U. S. Balance of Payments Position," *Factors Affecting the United States Balance of Payments*, Pt. 6, Joint Economic Committee, 87 Cong. 2 sess. (1962).

Note:

    r = rate of return (earnings) on total investment outstanding.

    a = proportion of earnings remitted as income to the United States.

    f = fees, royalties, etc., as a proportion of total direct investment outstanding.

    x = net exports as a proportion of total direct investment outstanding, i.e., exports minus imports.

    n.a. = not available.

    [a] Parameters are obtained by taking an average of the observed values of the items as defined for the years indicated. Data were obtained from U. S. Office of Business Economics, *Balance of Payments, Statistical Supplement Revised Edition* (1963).

    [b] Calculated for 1957–61.

sufficient data to make an estimate of the overall effect. This limitation is not as serious, however, as it might first appear. As shown in Table 4, areas outside of Europe account for most of the non-manufacturing direct investment in recent years. For these areas, many factors indicate that there is little difficulty in making the real transfer of resources from the United States equal the financial transfer of a direct investment.

In the first place, the capital equipment needed for the investment is seldom available locally and will probably be purchased in an advanced country—and very likely in the United States. Substantial purchases of the services of Americans are also made because trained nationals are scarce and U. S. technology is superior. Since the output of these investments is unlikely to compete with

U. S. domestic production, this negative factor will probably be relatively unimportant. Furthermore, earnings on these investments are likely to be great and repatriations generally are substantial. Finally, the less developed countries frequently find that the real barrier to their economic growth comes from a shortage of foreign exchange. Unless a financial transfer made to these countries is fully matched immediately by a flow of real resources from the United States or other countries, the excess would not be kept in idle reserves. These countries are too poor to save foreign exchange and, therefore, are likely to speed up their development efforts through greater imports as the availability of foreign exchange permits. Since Latin America, the area receiving the greatest amount of U. S. investment except for Canada and Europe, has especially close commercial ties with the United States, these funds will probably be spent in large measure in the United States. If Canada does not accumulate foreign reserves over time, investments in Canada act like investments in an underdeveloped country because of the exceedingly close integration of the U. S. and Canadian economies.

This suggests that investments in Europe are the ones most likely to cause serious balance-of-payments difficulties for the United States, and these investments are concentrated in petroleum refining and manufacturing. Petroleum refining investment in Europe is also unlikely to cause much trouble in the U. S. balance of payments. This is because the output does not compete with U. S. domestic production, and substantial earnings are made both directly from the operations and indirectly from the larger sales of crude petroleum by American-owned facilities in the Near East and North Africa. Thus, attention centers on manufacturing investment in Europe. And for this some estimates of the overall effect can be made.

Returns from Foreign Investment: Three Models

Any profitable investment from which some of the earnings are repatriated will eventually make the real transfer of resources equal to the financial transfer. Thus, the really interesting question is: How long will it take for the real transfer to be made? Estimates from three models based on different assumptions were calculated to see how long it might take to make the real transfer to Europe. The first model assumes that a single investment is undertaken and no others; the second model assumes that a new investment is undertaken and followed by new investments of identical size in subsequent years; and the third model assumes that a new investment is undertaken and that it marks the beginning of a flow of new investments that grows at a constant rate over time.

TABLE 7. Model 1: Estimated Balance-of-Payments Effects of a Single $1,000 Direct Investment in Manufacturing Facilities in Europe[a]

| | | Cumulative Direct | | | Repatri- | | Balance of Payments[b] | |
| Year | New Direct Investment | Investment End of Year | Export Stimulus | Royalties and Fees | ation Earnings | Import Stimulus | Annual Net Effect | Cumulative Effect |
	(1)	(2)	(3)	(4)	(5)	(6)	(7)	(8)
0	−1,000	1,000	0	0	0	0	−1,000	−1,000
1	0	1,081	106	23	87	−65	151	−849
2	0	1,169	115	24	94	−70	164	−685
3	0	1,264	124	26	102	−76	177	−508
4	0	1,366	134	29	110	−82	191	−317
5	0	1,477	145	31	119	−89	206	−111
6	0	1,597	157	33	128	−96	223	112
7	0	1,726	169	36	139	−104	241	353
8	0	1,865	183	39	150	−112	261	614
9	0	2,016	198	42	162	−121	282	896
10	0	2,179	214	46	175	−131	304	1,200

Note:
Column 2 = Column 2 for the preceding year plus 8.1 percent (retained earnings of current year).
Column 3 = 10.6 percent of investment (Column 2 of preceding year).
Column 4 = 2.3 percent of investment (Column 2 of preceding year).
Column 5 = 51.8 percent of total earnings, which are assumed to be 16.8 percent of investment making retained earnings 8.7 percent of investment (Column 2 of preceding year).
Column 6 = 6.5 percent of investment (Column 2 of preceding year).
Column 7 = Columns 1 + 3 + 4 + 5 + 6.
[a] It is assumed that the investment was made at the end of year 0.
[b] Excluding (1) related export stimulation; (2) American import replacement of foreign-owned production by American-owned production; and (3) displacement of U. S. exports by American-owned foreign production.

Estimates of the balance-of-payments effects of a single direct investment in European manufacturing are shown in Table 7.[16] These estimates should be considered suggestive not definitive. They are sensitive to the particular parameter values used—and, unfortunately, insufficient research has been devoted toward establishing these values. Furthermore, the stability of these parameters

[16] The estimates for all three tables use the parameters listed in Table 6.

over time and in the face of a tax change is open to question. However, these parameter values are the most appropriate ones now available for use in the calculations. The estimate indicates that the real transfer of resources to Europe made necessary by a new flow of funds from the United States is completed somewhere between the fifth and sixth year after the investment. By the end of the tenth year, the sum of the inflows to the United States is more than double the original outflow and the beneficial effects continue at a growing rate thereafter.

It is not possible to estimate all of the factors relevant to this calculation. In fact, this estimate overlooks four sets of forces, three of which would tend to strengthen the balance of payments and the other to weaken it. The estimate overlooks the fact that exports sold by the parent corporation through a trading subsidiary might also be aided by the existence of the foreign production facility. Furthermore, there is no estimate of the extent to which the goods imported by the United States from foreign subsidiaries would have been produced by a foreign firm without investment by American firms. To be specific, half of the imports from the foreign manufacturing subsidiaries of U. S. firms in Europe in the period investigated were automobiles.[17] Considering the demonstrated ability of foreign-owned firms to produce cars that are popular in the United States, this overstatement of import effects attributable to foreign investment may be significant. Moreover, new direct investment also helps maintain the profitability of existing foreign investment, although this effect cannot be measured.

Since no estimate was made of the loss of exports due to sales from foreign facilities, an important element weakening the balance of payments was not counted. (This is true also of the second and third models.) There is no way to judge the magnitude of this effect. It could be anywhere from zero to the total value of sales of manufacturing subsidiaries in Europe, which averaged around $8 billion per year for the years 1957–60, and exceeded $10 billion in 1961. Even if only a minor portion of these sales replaced American ex-

---

[17] Since the investigated period was the average of 1959 and 1960, the expected flow of imports may also have been overstated because of the atypical amount of foreign cars imported in 1959. See the survey provided by the Department of Commerce and presented in *President's 1961 Tax Recommendations*, Hearings before the House Ways and Means Committee, 87 Cong. 1 sess. (1961).

ports, the balance of payments was weakened considerably by such replacement.

The export component in production of foreign subsidiaries can be measured, however, where there is a somewhat greater possibility that they are replacing U. S. exports. In 1957, 18.6 percent of these sales were exports to countries other than the United States, with the United Kingdom the most important base for the export sales of American subsidiaries. Such a ratio of exports to total sales is no higher than is usual for British firms in similar industries; furthermore, all products made in Britain benefit from imperial preferences and preferential entry into EFTA countries. Automobiles alone represent 30 percent of the total sales of American-owned foreign subsidiaries, and clearly, the limitations on U. S. export of cars to Europe would have been great even without subsidiary competition. In the end, judgment of the impact of sales by foreign subsidiaries rests on the degree of choice available to businessmen and the choices made.

The results of the second model, in which a stream of new investment of constant amount is estimated, are shown in Table 8. The annual balance-of-payments impact remains negative until the sixth year, and the full adjustment to the new stream of investment would not be made until ten years after it had begun. This means that liquid dollar liabilities would build up in Europe for five years and then decrease, but would not be completely absorbed until ten years after the investment stream began. Because of the large increase in foreign investment coming from the new funds and retained earnings, a growing positive flow to the United States would continue after the real transfer was completed, and would be maintained until the investment was sold or otherwise liquidated.

Although the situation depicted in Model One would probably not cause much difficulty for the balance of payments since the reversal of the one-shot deterioration was begun immediately, there is no certainty that this is true of Model Two. The build-up of liquidity abroad for a period of five years might induce some foreign holders of dollar assets to convert them to gold. Any fear that the dollar would not maintain its value in the currency markets would be unwarranted considering the rapid increase in American-owned foreign assets and the resulting potential flows to the United

TABLE 8. Model 2: Estimated Balance-of-Payments Effects of a Flow of a $1,000 Direct Investment in Manufacturing Facilities in Europe[a]

Year	New Direct Investment (1)	Cumulative Direct Investment End of Year (2)	Export Stimulus (3)	Royalties and Fees (4)	Repatri- ation Earnings (5)	Import Stimulus (6)	Balance of Payments[b] Annual Net Effect (7)	Cumulative Effect (8)
0	−1,000	1,000	0	0	0	0	−1,000	−1,000
1	−1,000	2,081	106	23	87	−65	−849	−1,849
2	−1,000	3,250	221	48	181	−135	−685	−2,534
3	−1,000	4,513	345	75	283	−211	−508	−3,042
4	−1,000	5,879	478	104	393	−293	−318	−3,360
5	−1,000	7,355	623	135	511	−382	−113	−3,473
6	−1,000	8,951	780	169	640	−478	111	−3,362
7	−1,000	10,676	949	206	779	−582	352	−3,010
8	−1,000	12,541	1,132	246	929	−694	613	−2,397
9	−1,000	14,557	1,329	288	1,091	−815	893	−1,504
10	−1,000	16,736	1,543	335	1,266	−946	1,198	−306
11	−1,000	19,092	1,774	385	1,456	−1,088	1,527	1,221
12	−1,000	21,638	2,024	439	1,661	−1,241	1,883	3,104
13	−1,000	24,391	2,294	498	1,883	−1,406	2,269	5,373
14	−1,000	27,367	2,585	561	2,122	−1,585	2,683	8,056
15	−1,000	30,584	2,901	629	2,381	−1,779	3,132	11,188

Note:
Column 2 = Column 2 for the preceding year plus 8.1 percent (retained earnings of current year).
Column 3 = 10.6 percent of investment (Column 2 of preceding year).
Column 4 = 2.3 percent of investment (Column 2 of preceding year).
Column 5 = 51.8 percent of total earnings, which are assumed to be 16.8 percent of investment making retained earnings 8.7 percent of investment (Column 2 of preceding year).
Column 6 = 6.5 percent of investment (Column 2 of preceding year).
Column 7 = Columns 1 + 3 + 4 + 5 + 6.
[a] It is assumed that the investment was made at the end of year 0.
[b] Excluding (1) related export stimulation; (2) American import replacement of foreign-owned production by American-owned production; and (3) displacement of U. S. exports by American-owned foreign production.

States. But such a fear may still arise. The problem of the dollar in Model Two would be short-run liquidity, and if foreigners were not prepared to hold the dollars themselves, there is no reason to prevent the United States from using its gold stock for such purposes, since the stock would be replenished rather rapidly.

For Model Three, the amount of new investment from the United States was assumed to grow at an annual compound rate of 22 percent. While this rate may seem too high to be maintained, it is interesting to work out the exercise with what would seem to be an outside possibility, and this rate was the actual growth rate of

U. S. investment in European manufacturing between 1956 and 1961. The results of the third model are shown in Table 9. This situation is clearly different from those in the two previous models. Over the twenty-year period for which figures were calculated, the growth in return flows to the United States from previous investments was more than offset by the growth of new capital outflows

TABLE 9. Model 3: Estimated Balance-of-Payments Effects of a Growing Stream of Direct Investment in Manufacturing Facilities in Europe[a]

| | | Cumulative Direct | | | Repatri- | | Balance of Payments[b] | |
Year	New Direct Investment (1)	Investment End of Year (2)	Export Stimulus (3)	Royalties and Fees (4)	ation Earnings (5)	Import Stimulus (6)	Annual Net Effect (7)	Cumulative Effect (8)
0	−1,000	1,000	0	0	0	0	−1,000	−1,000
1	−1,220	2,301	106	23	87	−65	−1,069	−2,069
2	−1,488	3,975	244	53	200	−150	−1,141	−3,210
3	−1,815	6,112	421	91	346	−258	−1,215	−4,425
4	−2,214	8,821	648	141	532	−397	−1,290	−5,715
5	−2,701	12,237	935	203	767	−573	−1,369	−7,084
6	−3,295	16,523	1,297	281	1,065	−795	−1,447	−8,532
7	−4,020	21,881	1,751	380	1,437	−1,074	−1,526	−10,057
8	−4,904	28,557	2,319	503	1,904	−1,422	−1,600	−11,657
9	−5,983	36,853	3,027	657	2,484	−1,856	−1,671	−13,328
10	−7,299	47,137	3,906	848	3,206	−2,395	−1,734	−15,062
11	−8,905	59,860	4,997	1,084	4,101	−3,064	−1,787	−16,849
12	−10,864	75,573	6,345	1,377	5,208	−3,891	−1,825	−18,674
13	−13,254	94,948	8,011	1,738	6,575	−4,912	−1,842	−20,516
14	−16,170	118,809	10,064	2,184	8,260	−6,172	−1,834	−22,350
15	−19,727	148,160	12,594	2,733	10,336	−7,723	−1,787	−24,137
16	−24,067	184,228	15,705	3,408	12,890	−9,630	−1,694	−25,831
17	−29,362	228,512	19,528	4,237	16,028	−11,975	−1,544	−27,375
18	−35,822	282,843	24,222	5,256	19,881	−14,853	−1,316	−28,691
19	−43,703	349,456	29,981	6,505	24,607	−18,385	−995	−29,686
20	−53,318	431,080	37,042	8,037	30,403	−22,715	−551	−30,237

Note:
Column 2 = Column 2 for the preceding year plus 8.1 percent (retained earnings of current year).
Column 3 = 10.6 percent of investment (Column 2 of preceding year).
Column 4 = 2.3 percent of investment (Column 2 of preceding year).
Column 5 = 51.8 percent of total earnings, which are assumed to be 16.8 percent of investment making retained earnings 8.7 percent of investment (Column 2 of preceding year).
Column 6 = 6.5 percent of investment (Column 2 of preceding year).
Column 7 = Columns 1 + 3 + 4 + 5 + 6.
[a] It is assumed that the investment was made at the end of year 0.
[b] Excluding (1) related export stimulation; (2) American import replacement of foreign-owned production by American-owned production; and (3) displacement of U. S. exports by American-owned foreign production.

from the United States. After the thirteenth year, the negative impact begins to decline, but is not reversed. The cumulative deficit, equal to the increase in dollar liabilities held abroad, would be quite substantial and would constitute a serious problem. Despite the rapid growth of American-owned assets abroad, the build-up of U. S. liabilities would pose a threat to confidence in the dollar.

The balance-of-payments problem implied by Model Three is difficult to analyze. It is more than a short-run liquidity problem, since the deficit lasts for at least twenty years. Certainly the time required to absorb the liquidity generated by the investment would be longer than the planning horizon of officials who are obliged to manage U. S. currency. The possibility that foreign investment might raise this kind of problem leads to consideration of a tax change as an appropriate control mechanism. A change in the tax law making foreign investment less attractive would not only deter foreign investment immediately, it would also reduce the future stream of such investments.

Although the balance-of-payments problem implied by Model Three is a long-run one, this does not necessarily imply a fundamental disequilibrium in the world economy. The difficulty does not arise from any single foreign investment, but results from the cumulation of a growing stream of foreign investment. The resulting increase in foreign-held U. S. liabilities would become a problem as long as the growth of new foreign investment was expected to continue. If the capital flow were certain, foreigners might want to convert a major portion of their increases in international reserves into gold. With a reversal in the balance-of-payments position expected in the distant future, the United States might be unwilling to suffer the gold loss, or be unable to do so. Thus, a secondary wave of conversions of dollars to gold might occur if the promise of specie payment by the United States were doubted. Seen in this light, the problem is a long-run liquidity problem.

If the growth of new foreign investment from the United States could not be expected to continue with certainty, the countries of Europe receiving the U. S. investment would have to view their own balance-of-payments situations much differently. The European surplus position depends crucially on the constant injection of new capital flows from the United States. Prudence would dictate that the Europeans maintain sufficient reserves to protect themselves in the event that investment flows from the United States level off or decline. Suppose on the twentieth year (of Model Three) Americans decided to increase their investments in Europe only to the extent of their reinvested earnings (amounting to $28,306). The adverse balance of payments of Europe in that one year would then require greater reserves than had been accumulated in the previous nineteen years. Whether Europeans held their reserves in dollars or gold would still be a crucial matter, but since the potential claim on European reserves would be to cover dollar payments, dollars would probably be widely held.

How much concern the kind of balance-of-payments problem implied by Model Three should create depends on the realism of the Model's assumptions. The 1956–61 rate of growth of U. S. investment in European manufacturing facilities will probably not continue. Furthermore, as indicated earlier, that period was not typical from a number of points of view. Because this growth followed a period when U. S. investments in manufacturing facilities in Canada and Latin America had expanded greatly, in contrast to little in European manufacturing, the recent increase in European investment can be viewed as a catching-up process. In the second half of the fifties, economic growth in Europe continued while there was relative stagnation in the United States. If growth rates in Europe decline in the future, as is likely, and the U. S. rate increases, foreign investment will seem much less attractive—particularly now that U. S. tax laws provide a domestic investment credit not available for foreign investment. And should profit margins in Europe be narrowed because of cost-push factors, this tendency will be reinforced.

During this period, the birth of the two discriminatory trading organizations—EEC and EFTA—by offering tariff-saving possibilities, stimulated a burst of U. S. investment in Europe. This stimulus may subside in the future. Furthermore, the increased participation of U. S. ownership in the European economy implied by Model Three may not be feasible either politically or economically. So far, U. S. investment in Europe has been concentrated in only a few industries. If the rate assumed in the model is to continue, the number of firms undertaking foreign investment and the number of industries involved would have to expand. Such an event is unlikely. Undoubtedly the political opposition to U. S. control of European industries would increase and might well lead to restrictive action from the European side. Finally, a view of the 1950–62 figures themselves gives the impression of a movement from one level of investment, 1950–55, to a higher one, 1960–62 (Model Two), instead of a steady rate of growth (Model Three).

All three models were directed to investment in European manufacturing facilities because this type of investment is crucial. A calculation of Model One for investment in manufacturing facilities in Latin America indicates that the real transfer is completed in the second year after investment. For investment in Canada, the corresponding calculation indicates that the real transfer is completed between the fourth and fifth year. The application of Models Two and Three to Latin America and Canada also indicates that a much shorter time is needed to cover a transfer than in Europe.

Conclusions

General economic reasoning leads to the conclusion that tax neutrality between domestic and foreign investments is desirable from a world point of view. Neutrality promotes the most efficient world-wide distribution of capital and thereby maximizes world welfare. Increasing world welfare can be considered consistent with national welfare in the long run. The United States should, therefore, seek domestic neutrality, unless it is inconsistent with other more basic goals of public policy. Other goals that could be affected are the stimulation of domestic growth, the stimulation of growth in certain foreign countries, and the maintenance—or achievement—of a healthy balance-of-payments position for the United States.

In practice, however, domestic tax neutrality is difficult to achieve. The requirements for theoretical neutrality are fairly clear. In the absence of any distortions in the world economy, domestic tax neutrality can be approached by: (1) enforcing the same tax rate on income wherever earned; (2) having the tax liability arise when the income is earned; and (3) allowing a full tax credit for income taxes paid to a foreign government. The practical difficulties in achieving domestic tax neutrality are caused by the necessity of compensating for a number of real differences in the situations under which foreign and domestic firms operate. Among these are differences in: the definition of taxable income between areas, allowable tax credits, the level and incidence of other types of taxes, and governmental services. In addition, there is the need to compensate for monopoly and other distorting influences in the world economy.

The existing tax laws of the United States depart from domestic neutrality in two ways; some encourage, and others discourage, foreign investment. Current laws also discriminate as between foreign areas by allowing special privileges to investment within the Western Hemisphere. On balance, it appears as if an approximate position of domestic tax neutrality may well exist between the United States and those countries whose effective income tax rates are only slightly below the U. S. rates. When the effective income tax rate is substantially below (or above) the U. S. rate, domestic neutrality is probably not present. And it certainly is not present, nor even attempted, for investment in countries given special tax privileges by the United States.

Although domestic tax neutrality may be desirable, it is clearly not the only consideration relevant to the formation of appropriate tax legislation. Other goals of public policy can and possibly should be served by the tax laws. As a goal of public policy, the United States encourages the economic development of the less developed countries. If it is assumed that U. S. foreign investment in underdeveloped countries does aid their economic development, tax incentives may be needed to increase this investment. In fact, as described earlier, the United States already encourages such investment through use of the Western Hemisphere Trading Corporation and through certain rules embodied in the Revenue Act of 1962. And such tax inducements would be substantially broadened if the recent recommendations of the Commerce Committee for the Alliance for Progress (COMAP) were adopted.[18] The COMAP recommendations are especially far-reaching and could well have a marked effect on domestic neutrality, as well as the other economic factors considered in this study.

[18] See Chapter II for summary of the proposed tax changes, based on COMAP, *Proposals to Improve the Flow of U. S. Private Investment to Latin America* (March 1963).

An investment tax credit up to the limit allowed on domestic investment, generally 7 percent, would probably tend to promote domestic neutrality. However, an investment tax credit for as much as 25 percent or 30 percent (as proposed by COMAP) would constitute a gross departure from domestic neutrality and would probably lead to a misallocation of world capital resources. It thus must be defended on other grounds.[19] A tax certificate such as COMAP proposed to guarantee a minimum level of return on foreign investment might have desirable aspects if it existed but was never used in practice; for then it would merely serve to counter the illusion of risk. Relieving an investor of the real risk of low profits, however, can only promote an inefficient allocation of scarce resources. Risk illusion might be effectively countered by a low-cost insurance program such as the one recommended in the COMAP report. Tax sparing would also constitute a gross departure from domestic neutrality with the same possible consequences. In addition, tax sparing might encourage an undesirable repatriation of earnings and capital (as recognized in the COMAP report), and would force the less developed countries to compete for foreign investment by eroding their own tax base. Since underdeveloped countries are likely to need an expansion, rather than a contraction, of governmental revenues, an erosion of their tax base would be a serious matter.

A tax credit for foreign exchange losses caused by currency devaluation would also depart from domestic neutrality. Devaluation losses differ considerably from the kinds of losses that are a deduction (not a credit) from taxable income on domestic investment. This is because devaluation, in most cases, results from price inflation, which yields expanded money profits as well as losses for investment. It would not be neutral to take away the burden of all losses of inflation from the firm without taking all the profits that also result from the inflation. Neither would expansion of the tax deferral privilege through a new corporate form be neutral, since tax deferral is nonneutral in itself, and would clearly not be neces-

---

[19] One can argue that investments in underdeveloped countries yield social benefits outside the firm; therefore, social returns to investment are greater than private returns, and incentives to invest in these countries may not lead to a maldistribution of world capital.

sary to compensate for departures from domestic neutrality in the other direction. Finally, the allowance of foreign investment losses against U. S. income taxes would promote domestic neutrality if similar allowances were given for losses on domestic investment. Anything more generous would be nonneutral. In summary, if enacted, the group of recommendations contained in the COMAP report would as a whole constitute a great departure from domestic tax neutrality.

This analysis of foreign tax neutrality led to the conclusion that such neutrality in fact cannot be achieved, since U. S. foreign operations face competition from nationals of more than one country, each of whom has a separate tax system. Furthermore, an approach toward foreign tax neutrality would appear to be counter to the needs of domestic tax neutrality. The very existence of overlapping tax jurisdictions appears to make this an insoluble problem.

We concluded from our analysis of the equity issue that the existing tax laws, without the deferral privilege, are not equitable between domestic operations and foreign subsidiaries. We also concluded that U. S. tax laws are not equitable, and cannot be made equitable, between U. S. foreign subsidiaries and their competitors on foreign soil. In fact, the only possibility for achieving equity seems to be among U. S. foreign subsidiaries operating in the same foreign country.

The proposals of the COMAP report would tend to undermine even the degree of equity existing among U. S. foreign subsidiaries themselves. They would tend to lighten the tax burden only on new foreign investment to the exclusion of existing foreign investment in order to prevent windfall profits, but this would destroy the equity that does exist.

Foreign investment under conditions of full employment, we believe, probably would lead to a diminution of domestic economic growth to the degree that real resources were transferred from domestic to foreign uses. This happens because it is likely that repatriated foreign earnings could not sufficiently stimulate domestic investment to compensate for the loss of investment coming from a smaller stream of domestic output. However, if there are unused resources available in the U. S. economy of the type needed by foreign subsidiaries, foreign investment need not deter domestic growth, and may promote it.

From the point of view of domestic growth, the increase in foreign investment that would result if the COMAP proposals were adopted may be desirable if there exists unused capacity in the U. S. economy. Few, if any, bottleneck problems would arise and other complications would probably not occur since the resulting output would not be very competitive with U. S. output. There is a question, however, whether this is the best use to be made of excess capacity.

We have reached no firm conclusions on the effect of foreign investment on the U. S. balance of payments. The difficulty in reaching conclusions results from the theoretical problem of comparing the actual situation of having foreign investments to a hypothetical situation without them, and because of a lack of data on the actual situation. At best, we could only determine a type of ranking of foreign investments—a ranking moving from those least likely to those most likely to cause balance-of-payments problems. The foreign investments least likely to cause balance-of-payments problems are those used to develop natural resources and to develop commercial outlets for U. S. exports, and those centered in countries with especially close economic ties with the United States, such as Canada and Latin American countries. The investments that could cause difficulties for the United States are those that expand the manufacturing capacity for the production of goods competitive with U. S. domestic output, especially those made in Europe.

We speculated on the basis of incomplete data that an isolated investment in a European manufacturing facility was not likely to cause difficulty. A real problem might arise, however, if a constant stream of U. S. investment in European manufacturing facilities began; and the problem would be even greater if such a stream grew. The nature of the balance-of-payments problem involved, however, does not appear to be a fundamental disequilibrium requiring a change in the exchange rate, but a liquidity problem. If a constant stream of investment causes the difficulty, a short-run liquidity problem might arise, which presumably could be handled with existing defenses of the dollar. If there were a growing stream of investment, a long-run liquidity problem might occur. Even this problem might not be too serious because the need for holding international liquidity would be created in the very countries accumulating the liquid dollar claims.

If foreign investment were increased in Latin America as a result of enactment of the COMAP proposals, it is highly unlikely that a balance-of-payments problem would result. The real transfer of resources to Latin America is generally made in an exceedingly short period of time. In fact, the U. S. balance of payments might be improved if the investments lead to outputs in Latin America that replace imports formerly coming from Europe (or from economies which are closely integrated with Europe), or if they lead to greater Latin American exports to Europe. The COMAP proposals, therefore, probably would undermine domestic tax neutrality and tax equity, but under conditions of unemployment, might stimulate U. S. domestic growth and improve the U. S. balance of payments. Helping the less developed countries is a goal of public policy primarily because of the resulting political gains, and it is not at all clear that the United States would obtain those gains by adopting a policy that implied that the United States was exporting domestic unemployment.

It is clear from the foregoing that the analysis of the effects of the taxation of foreign-earned income is not one of the easy problems of economics. It involves international trade theory, income and price theory, as well as public finance theory. The analysis abounds with both theoretical and empirical problems. Indeed, when recommendations in this area are weighed, the international political problems should also be analyzed. However, research in this neglected area has begun, and we hope that it will be continued.

CHAPTER V

Summary of Conference Discussion

THE ECONOMIC AND POLITICAL conditions that lead to the foreign-source income provisions of the Revenue Act of 1962 were very much in the minds of the participants of the conference, and, therefore, the issues discussed were mainly those previously raised in connection with the legislation. The topics discussed included: (1) the background of the Revenue Act of 1962; (2) tax principles relevant to the taxation of corporate income; (3) the effect of taxes on foreign investment; (4) the consequences of foreign investment for domestic economic growth; (5) the implications of foreign investment for the balance of payments; (6) a critique of the Revenue Act of 1962; and (7) possible changes in the taxation of foreign-source income.

For purposes of brevity, no attempt has been made to summarize all statements made at the conference. It is, therefore, especially important to note that an unchallenged statement does not necessarily imply general agreement by the group. As announced at the conference, the proponents of particular points of view are not identified. The order of material in this summary does not necessarily correspond to the order of discussion in the conference.

The Background of the Revenue Act of 1962

In 1961 and 1962 many prevailing conditions prompted a basic review of the United States position on taxing foreign income. In the preceding years, there had been a rather determined effort to obtain tax preferences to promote foreign investment, but no legislation was enacted. But by 1961, there was also general concern over the balance-of-payments position of the United States, and it was thought that additional foreign investment might conflict with, at least, short-term needs of the balance of payments. A review of the tax treatment of foreign income was begun during the Eisenhower Administration, and it was resumed by the Treasury under the Kennedy Administration. The review was quite comprehensive and included the taxation of foreign-source income of individuals, foreign trusts, foreign investment companies, foreign real estate as well as foreign-source corporate income. This may well have been the first such review ever undertaken by the United States or indeed by any government within recent years. The task was made more difficult because lawyers, accountants, and economists had tended to neglect this area of research.

After a thorough but hurried study, the Treasury concluded that tax equity should be an important guide for tax policy and that domestic neutrality (treating foreign subsidiaries identically to domestic producers) should provide the yardstick against which taxing practices should be measured. The Treasury thought the tax treatment of foreign-source income prior to the 1962 tax law was too liberal and preferential compared to domestic investment. It also decided that the deterrence of foreign investment that might result from the removal of the existing tax preferences for such investment was consistent with short-run needs of the balance of payments and, therefore, was not in conflict with nontax policies. Moreover, the Treasury felt that changes in the tax law were required of themselves and not merely as a means of improving the balance of payments. Presumably, if the tax changes were not consistent with short-term balance-of-payments requirements, the movement toward the long-run tax goal would have been delayed. Certainly the Congress would not support changes in the law to meet long-run tax goals if they were inconsistent with immediate policy needs.

As to the proposals, the Treasury had to decide between recommending the complete elimination of deferral in the case of American-owned foreign subsidiaries or merely suggesting legislation to meet problems of aggravated deferral—essentially the tax-haven problem (the legal device that drains taxable income from a high tax country to a low tax country). It decided to propose the complete elimination of deferral for investment in developed countries as the best and simplest solution, but to continue deferral for investment in underdeveloped countries, as consistent with United States policy of encouraging investment in these areas. As it later turned out, tax-haven legislation alone was acceptable to the Treasury in the event the Congress would not accept complete elimination of deferral.

The business community was shocked by the Treasury recommendations. In early 1961, it still believed the government wanted to stimulate foreign investment and was considering granting further tax concessions instead of withdrawing them. Businessmen considered the one hundred and eighty degree shift in U. S. policy all the more mystifying since they felt that the recommendations raised new barriers to the flow of international capital that were inconsistent with all of U. S. postwar tax and economic policy. The business community raised a determined assault against the Treasury recommendations and convinced the Congress that complete elimination of deferral was too extreme.

The Congress was prepared, however, to legislate against tax havens. Having abandoned the simpler solution of completely eliminating deferral, the resulting legislation necessarily became very complex. The Treasury was put in the position of having to find an acceptable middle ground while still fighting for its prime target. Since the area of tax-haven legislation was completely novel, it was necessary to traverse wholly new legal terrain. The many different pressures in the Congress pushing in several directions worked against a simple solution. The resulting legislation was considered by some observers as the best compromise in these circumstances.

Tax Principles

Many problems concerning the "rightness" or "wrongness" of a tax solution are difficult to solve, since there may not be agreement on what is the correct tax principle to apply, or the several relevant principles may themselves yield conflicting policy recommendations. The Treasury's decision to elevate domestic neutrality to a commanding position was not accepted by many analysts who thought that foreign neutrality (having the United States treat its foreign subsidiaries the same way foreign governments treat their corporations) as a principle should stand on at least an equal footing with domestic neutrality. Most of the argument is contained in the records of the hearings before the congressional tax-writing committees. It was reviewed and subjected to detailed scrutiny at the conference.

The opinion was expressed that foreign neutrality, not domestic neutrality, should be the guiding principle for taxing foreign-source income. If foreign neutrality were not recognized, American businesses operating abroad would be at a disadvantage compared to their foreign-owned competitors. It was argued that higher corporate income taxes resulting from, say, the elimination of deferral would mean more than a reduction of income to corporate stockholders. Taxes that fall on profits are becoming less distinct from taxes that enter as elements in costs. If a portion or all of the corporate income tax is shifted, American-owned businesses abroad will be at a disadvantage in competition with foreign competitors. The choice is not between serving the market with exports from domestic plants or serving the market from foreign-based American plants, but between United States participation through American-owned foreign plants or withdrawal from foreign markets. It was stated that, in many cases, the only way to get the foreign business was to have a foreign plant.

It was argued that the advantage of moving toward foreign neutrality would be, first of all, an increase in world welfare and, particularly, a more rapid development of the less developed countries. From the point of view of the United States, American firms would be better able to compete abroad, thereby earning high rates of profits and foreign exchange. The U. S. economy also would gain from the collateral and ancillary benefits of foreign investment. Furthermore, it was claimed that some foreign governments would resent the fact that the U. S. Treasury would receive a tax on income earned in their countries and might seek ways to discriminate against American firms in order to capture this tax revenue for themselves. While the critics supporting foreign neutrality recognized the difficulty of adjusting American taxing practices to those of a number of foreign countries whose practices themselves differ, they believed that it would be possible to determine a common tax practice used by the major capital exporting countries. In particular, it was noted that all foreign countries allow the deferral of taxes on foreign-source income until the time of repatriation.

It was further mentioned that even with much more liberal U. S. tax laws, American firms may find competition with foreign-owned firms difficult because American firms tend to pay their foreign taxes in full. Therefore, even if the same tax rate applied universally, American firms would suffer because they refuse to adopt some of the methods used by foreign competitors to avoid taxes. Moreover, unlike foreign-owned firms, American firms are prevented by the Revenue Act of 1962 from enjoying reduced foreign taxes through use of tax havens. There seems to be no concrete evidence to support the common belief that foreign firms do not use the base-company device very frequently, and there is some evidence that they do. In general, it is next to impossible to obtain information about how foreign-owned firms, especially family-held businesses, handle their tax affairs. In view of these disadvantages, it was argued that American-owned foreign operations should not be burdened further.

Much of the foregoing was disputed by those who upheld domestic neutrality as the appropriate goal of policies in this field. While restrictions on the competitive ability of American-owned foreign subsidiaries was not endorsed as an end in itself, the opinion was expressed that such a result must be accepted if required to avoid discrimination against American domestic investment. If domestic neutrality is not sought in U. S. tax laws, low foreign tax rates may place American firms operating at home at a disadvantage in competition with American-owned foreign subsidiaries. The difference in rates could be important in the competition for foreign markets where subsidiaries are operating, for third country export markets, and even for the domestic market if foreign subsidiaries export back to the United States. This disadvantage would tend to inhibit domestic investment and to attract American investment abroad artificially, which in turn might have the further side effect of intensifying the short-term balance-of-payments problem of the United States. In fact, it was argued that domestic neutrality is the only valid tax principle because the comparison of domestic to foreign tax rates alone can influence U. S. international capital flows.

The disadvantage to domestic investment comes about through the deferral mechanism. In those cases where the effective foreign tax rate is close to the U. S. rates, not much disadvantage is involved. However, when deferral is combined with a low foreign tax rate in the country of operations or when otherwise higher foreign taxes in the country of operations can be avoided through a tax-haven device, the situation is aggravated. Even the existence of low foreign tax rates in the country of operations may not be too serious since countries that have enacted low rates generally are compensating for other economic shortcomings, and American investment is influenced by the totality of the foreign economic situation, not by taxes alone. If this were not the case and low rates were found in Japan or the advanced countries of Europe, for example, the Congress would probably have been more receptive to the complete elimination of deferral.

The tax-haven situation, therefore, was considered the most critical problem requiring legislative action in 1962. This problem accounts for the Treasury's willingness to compromise on such a solution. Even though the taxes avoided were those of foreign countries rather than those of the United States, this type of aggravated deferral was attacked because of the fear that substantial amounts of American capital were being artificially attracted abroad at the expense of domestic investment. The tax-haven device was also being used to drain income that should have been attributed to domestic activities and, therefore, some U. S. tax revenues were being lost, and the Treasury sought to prevent this practice.

If domestic neutrality is accepted as the primary tax principle, the difficulty of taking into account a multitude of foreign tax practices is avoided, and if extended to the complete elimination of deferral, a less complex solution would emerge. Many difficulties of interpretation would still remain, however, and some new ones would be introduced. Suppose foreign income is taxed when earned; a problem would arise if the foreign currency in which the income is earned is subsequently depreciated or appreciated. Presumably, some adjustment would have to be made for the change in the value of previous foreign earnings that had not been repatriated. The amount of the adjustment and its timing would pose quite a problem. Furthermore, it could be argued that the entire tax situation facing the subsidiary abroad compared to the entire tax situation in the United States would have to be evaluated to ensure a balanced interpretation of domestic neutrality and the approach, therefore, is also imprecise. Moreover, factors other than taxes, such as exchange and capital controls and financial differences, would have to be weighed in the neutrality determination.

Opposition was even expressed by some conference participants to tax-haven legislation. When it is directed against reduction of foreign income taxes, it was argued that foreign countries have ample power to prevent the abuse of their tax systems via tax havens and that the United States has insufficient reason in doing this for them. When American firms employ base companies, they merely use tax differences to their advantage, just as tax differences between states in the United States are used. The discouragement of base companies may also reduce the ultimate tax revenues of the United States, since foreign earnings, when repatriated, will carry with them a larger tax credit for foreign taxes paid than otherwise. It was also stated that no other country recognizes domestic neutrality as a primary principle for taxing foreign-source income, although it was also stated that some European countries are concerned about the tax-haven problems they face.

The debate between the proponents of domestic neutrality and the advocates of foreign neutrality may have been overshadowed in the Congress by notions of equity. In fact, several participants thought that equity was given much more weight in the congressional discussions than the background study indicates. The difficulty in determining what equity required in this field was overlooked in the Congress because taxing practices prior to 1962 seemed to violate a basic idea of fairness. The Congress was impressed because some foreign subsidiaries earning a great deal of money through the use of tax havens were able to avoid paying any substantial amount of taxes to any government, and the Congress did not want to let this situation continue.

Congressional attitudes were supported by a number of so-called "horror stories" of tax abuses arising from the use of foreign-based companies. Initially, those tax havens designed to shift for tax purposes an abnormal amount of American-earned income abroad were considered most important because they involved an evasion of U. S. taxes. This device was profitable since the artificially generated foreign income was sheltered by the deferral mechanism and furthermore the funds might never be repatriated. Subsequently, Congress also concerned itself with tax havens into which income earned in foreign countries was being sent to avoid paying foreign taxes. The Congress, feeling that it was immoral not to be paying taxes to someone, also opposed this device. While Congress recognized that the deferral mechanism makes these abuses possible, it drew a sharp distinction between those cases in which deferral gave only small benefits, and those, as in tax havens, in which it gave very substantial gains. It was prepared to act only against the latter.

The Effect of Taxes on Foreign Investment

Early in the conference discussion, the point was made that the attitude that United States tax laws should take in reference to foreign investment depends crucially on how large the foreign investment might be in the future and what effect the tax laws would have on it. This latter question was discussed and the consensus appeared to be that, in general, taxes were not the major factor in determining foreign investment. Many other factors appeared to be more important than taxes in influencing the decision of businessmen to produce abroad. Conversely, it was noted that taxes were rarely mentioned by businessmen as a reason their foreign ventures failed to prosper. It therefore appears that the tax changes embodied in the Revenue Act of 1962 will not greatly affect the aggregate of foreign investment.

This is not to suggest that taxes have no impact on foreign investment. It was observed that high taxes may be quite important in dissuading small and medium-sized firms from attempting foreign investment. Furthermore, taxes might have a disproportionate weight in the decision of a firm that is considering its first foreign venture. Tax rates can be observed and are definite while some other potentially more important factors, such as conditions in the labor market and marketing outlets, are much less visible. Firms with experience abroad are better able to weigh these more important factors. Finally, tax considerations might be important in deciding how much foreign income to repatriate in dividends to parent corporations, and how much to reinvest abroad in foreign subsidiaries. When taxes are important, depreciation guidelines and investment credits as well as nominal tax rates are influential.

Foreign Investment and Domestic Economic Growth

If the provisions for taxing foreign-source income have little effect on foreign investment, they cannot be very important in determining domestic economic growth, particularly in view of the belief that the contribution of marginal changes in domestic investment to domestic growth is rather small. Nevertheless, the discussion of the relationship between foreign investment and domestic growth was interesting. The distinction was drawn between growth of gross national product (GNP) and growth of gross domestic product (GDP). The former can be favorably influenced by high rates of return on foreign investment while the latter is restricted to income generated at home.

The effect of foreign investment on the growth of gross domestic product depends on the consequences of foreign investment for domestic investment, which in turn is related to the utilization rate of domestic factors of production. The background study presents the view that foreign investment need not inhibit domestic investment if there is less than full use of resources at home, but would inhibit the growth of gross domestic product in the event of full employment. A different view presented at the conference was that the domestic growth consequences of foreign investment would be really unimportant if the government was following a full employment monetary and fiscal policy. However, if there were unemployment, foreign investment could constrain the adoption of proper government policies, even though it might not directly inhibit domestic investment. As a counter example to this view, it was suggested that in periods of severe depression like the 1930's, even an embargo on foreign investment would not have increased domestic investment and might have had the reverse effect.

On a less aggregative level, it was questioned whether a firm deciding to make a foreign investment does not thereby forego a corresponding domestic investment. It was argued that decision for a foreign investment is similar to a decision to put up a plant in Texas which precludes building one in New York. A firm needs only so much productive capacity to serve its market and also has a limited amount of financing for investment.

This opinion was opposed on a number of grounds. It was argued that the only way to get business is to produce where the market is situated—and thus, if a firm builds a foreign plant, it does not replace a domestic investment. If a firm finds a good investment opportunity at home and also one abroad, it will probably make both investments, not one or the other. Financing a good investment prospect is seldom a problem because of ample internal funds and the ease of going into the capital market for funds. The real constraint on domestic investment is thought to be the lack of good investment opportunities at home, resulting from the limits of the domestic market and the paucity of exploitable research. For medium-sized firms, insufficient management personnel may also be a constraint. Most firms view their investment decisions as a choice in the use of funds. They are under little direct pressure to raise dividends as a percentage of earnings, and they are not inclined to do so. They will invest in their own line of business at home until they can no longer increase their share of the market. They then choose either to diversify their business in order to make further domestic investment or to stay in the same business and invest abroad. What appears as an alternative to the firm, however, is not one for the economy as a whole, since if one firm chooses not to diversify, the investment opportunity can be absorbed by some other firm.

The Balance-of-Payments Implications of Foreign Investment

Although the relationship between foreign investment and the balance of payments has been the subject of extensive debate, the conference discussion pointed up how little is still known about this relationship. Tables 7, 8, and 9 of the background study, which attempted to approximate this relationship under different assumptions, were subjected to a searching and critical examination. The discussion of the assumptions—a single foreign investment, a stream of foreign investments of constant size, or a rapidly growing foreign investment stream—led to the conclusion that the actual situation probably corresponds to a position mid-way between a constant and rapidly growing stream. There is no assurance, however, that the magnitudes indicated in the tables are correct.

The difficulties involved in interpreting Tables 7, 8, and 9 include problems of omission and commission. It was observed that the time required to make new investment effective is not recognized. Unfortunately, it is impossible to make an estimate of the time interval from aggregative data, and the information is not available from company reports since firms do not want this information made public. The interval for existing foreign enterprises, however, may be much less than for new ones.

New foreign investment often reinforces existing foreign investment, and this effect on profits is not recognized in the tables. Continuous investment is required to maintain existing plants and safeguard the competitive position of firms in the markets in which they operate. Thus, new investment not only earns a return, it also maintains the return on old investment. Furthermore, the tables assume a constant percentage of import and export stimulation throughout the life of the investment, This assumption is very weak because both forms of stimulation probably lessen over time. Moreover, the assumption of a constant repatriation ratio is questionable. Essentially, the amount of repatriated earnings results from an internal struggle within firms. Foreign managers are often empire builders and do not want to repatriate anything. However, comptrollers who have to make a debt service on funds borrowed for foreign operations, and who also need to provide funds for dividends to stockholders, want to receive funds for these purposes from their foreign subsidiaries. Also, some nonconsolidated firms want the profits of foreign subsidiaries to appear in reports of company earnings, and this requires repatriation. It is by no means certain that the struggle will yield a constant repatriation ratio over time.

Although the background paper recognizes some relevant variables not included in the estimates, it fails to mention others. United States investment in some foreign countries may have a noticeable impact on the national income of those countries that is ultimately reflected in American exports and imports. Also, the direct impact of the receipt of U. S. funds on the balance of payments in some countries may substantially influence their behavior. These effects may be most pronounced for the less developed countries. Furthermore, the relevant variables for which estimates could not be made may be as important as those included. The displacement of U. S. exports by new U. S. foreign investment, for example, could be very significant. The opinion was expressed that the level of foreign import barriers was so substantial that exports cannot be substituted for direct investment. However, in some cases, such as the U. S. investment induced by the Canadian incentive scheme to invest in Canada to produce automobile parts, pure substitution results. In general, there seemed to be little confidence in the rough estimates of the background study, although there was no consensus as to the direction in which they most likely err.

Only a negative policy implication could be abstracted from the balance-of-payments discussion. From the point of view of the long-run balance of payments, tax policy should neither encourage nor discourage direct foreign investment. Thus principles of equity and neutrality alone provide ground for long-run policy determination. This should not suggest, however, that neutrality can never be consciously violated if sufficient justification appears. Particularly in the short run, tax policy could be nonneutral to serve other policy goals. The short-run policy position regarding foreign investment depends on whether the balance of payments can stand the strain during the years of increasing foreign investment until the return flows build up to offset them.

Critique of the Revenue Act of 1962

Viewed from outside the government, the foreign-source income provisions of the Revenue Act of 1962 seemed to have five purposes in the field of foreign-source income: (1) to curtail the massive increase in foreign direct investment for reasons of the balance of payments; (2) to divert investment from developed to less developed countries without considering the balance of payments; (3) to prevent the artificial diversion of foreign income from high to low tax countries; (4) to prevent the artificial diversion of domestic income to low-tax foreign countries in order to bolster U. S. revenues; (5) to eliminate tax preferences that artificially impeded the repatriation of income from abroad. In addition, the general purpose of the act was to promote equity and domestic neutrality. The opinion was expressed that the act served only the fourth of the specific objectives and, in general, did not substantially change the neutrality situation. Others thought that the third objective was also served.

The act immediately encouraged a number of firms to eliminate their foreign-base companies, without ceasing operations abroad. In a small number of instances, it might even have induced firms to begin production abroad if in the past they were using foreign-base companies to absorb export profits. The export trade corporation provision was written to avoid this possibility, but opinions differed whether the definitions used in the provision were sufficiently broad to achieve this objective.

Some participants argued that in part the act works at cross purposes. On the one hand, it is intended to stimulate investment in the less developed countries, while on the other, it prevents the direct shifting of funds from subsidiaries in developed countries to those in less developed countries and thereby works in the opposite direction. Furthermore, one desirable feature of foreign-base companies was lost. Previously, funds could be pooled from diverse sources and invested independently of tax considerations. Now tax differences between foreign countries will affect investment decisions and presumably misallocate capital, although it is still possible to pool funds among the less developed countries.

The whole area of tax administration for foreign-source income was critically discussed. Because of its complexity and the difficulty of audit, there have been substantial delays in getting tax returns accepted under the law prior to 1962. Since the Revenue Act of 1962 has increased the complexity of the law, it was argued that the cost of compliance has been raised considerably, and will work a hardship on small and medium-sized firms. It was recognized that administration in this field is difficult; moreover, it was pointed out that not all the difficulty can be attributed to the law itself. Local agents have become more sophisticated and are now unwilling to accept on faith many figures that were previously not questioned because too many liberties had been taken under the old system. The new law is complex, and the regulations for guiding agents in the field are not yet fully issued. This situation is being remedied, and administration certainly will not break down. It was also noted that other countries than the United States have administrative difficulties in this field.

Some critics felt that accepting the continuation of deferral in return for prohibitions against tax havens could not be supported by any single policy theory. The situation is made even worse by the overlaying of the export trade corporation provision. Furthermore, it was argued that worry about one source of aggravated deferral, tax havens, without worry about low foreign tax rates was inconsistent. It was noted that low tax rates can be found even in Western Europe for special situations such as tax holidays and depressed area schemes.

It was suggested that non-tax-haven deferral problems are less important today than in 1961. In the first place, U. S. tax rates have been reduced. Also depreciation guidelines have been liberalized, and the investment credit has been added (available only for domestic investment). Thus there is less potential U. S. claim for taxes on foreign-source earnings. The act, in reaching only the aggravated tax-haven deferral aspect, was defended not only as being the best compromise, given the congressional situation, but also as a highly desirable piece of legislation.

Possible Future Changes in the Tax Law

During the conference, a number of proposals for changing the provisions for the taxation of foreign-source income were discussed. Alternatively, it was suggested that a moratorium be called on all tax changes in order to accumulate enough experience to evaluate the current law and to provide time for more careful analysis by lawyers and economists. Four types of policy proposals were considered, including proposals to find alternative methods of achieving the goals of the current law, proposals to raise the effective level of taxation, proposals to reduce the level of U. S. taxes, and proposals to find ways of avoiding international chaos in taxation.

Even if one accepts the goal of the Revenue Act of 1962 of seeking a middle ground between complete elimination of deferral without escape and the pre-existing situation, one may still question the method chosen. It was suggested that a minimum distribution approach, building on the minimum distribution alternative included in the 1962 act respecting tax havens, might provide a better way to reach a middle ground solution. This would require that deferral be eliminated unless a firm conformed to a minimum distribution schedule, with the schedule relating the minimum repatriation ratio to the difference between the U. S. tax rate and the rates of the country of operations. In essence, this scheme would determine a minimum immediate overall tax rate (domestic and foreign) that would apply to all foreign earnings. One advantage of this approach would be simplicity. It is much easier to eliminate deferral and then allow exceptions than to start the other way around as in the 1962 act. This method would also allow the pooling of foreign earnings rather than a country-by-country approach. Furthermore, it would attack all cases of aggravated deferral, not just tax havens. However, a problem would arise from this approach because of the distortion of average levels of taxes that comes from the inclusion of capital gains and losses. Moreover, this approach would still be subject to all the criticisms against ending deferral that are implied in the concept of foreign neutrality.

Still another approach to the middle ground would be to urge all firms to organize their foreign operations as special forms of domestic corporations similar to Western Hemisphere Trade Corporations. One could make concessions on the tax rate and even have different rates between developed and less developed countries if that were thought desirable. The advantages suggested for this approach would be that deferral would be completely eliminated, and the barrier against repatriation of foreign earnings would be destroyed. With any form of deferral, foreign earnings on which large potential U. S. tax claims exist are locked in abroad and may never be repatriated. As domestic corporations, they could be taxed directly, thus avoiding the awkward indirect method. The problems with this approach would also be very great. The loss of the substantial advantage of being a foreign resident when conducting business abroad would hurt the competitive position of U. S. firms. Foreign participation also might prove difficult if a U. S. corporation rather than a foreign corporation were used.

On the basis of a strict interpretation of domestic neutrality, it was suggested that all deferral be eliminated. This proposal would make no exception for less developed countries. The elimination of deferral on earnings in less developed countries was defended on the ground that deferral was not a good method of reaching United States policy objectives in these areas. Since the arguments for and against this position were all known to the participants, no further discussion was required.

Diametrically opposed to the last proposal was the suggestion that foreign neutrality be elevated to a primary position. Most foreign governments are very liberal in the treatment they afford the foreign income of their business firms and allow tax deferral, base companies and, in some cases, exclusion of foreign income from domestic taxation. Thus, if American foreign subsidiaries are not going to be at a competitive disadvantage, the United States should also consider excluding foreign-source income in whole or in part from domestic taxation. Exclusion from domestic taxation was not endorsed as a desirable end in itself, but was reluctantly recognized as the only way to ensure that U. S. firms would be treated like their foreign competitors. Since the arguments for and against this position were equally well known, further discussion was again unnecessary.

It was recognized that if all countries attempted to match each tax concession granted by any foreign country to its domestic firms on foreign-source income, taxation in this field could become chaotic. It was argued, however, that the United States is unlikely to prevent chaos by taking unilateral tax leadership because other countries are unlikely to follow. The United States, by restricting the action of American business firms unilaterally, may have lost its bargaining ability to induce other countries to become more responsible. However, some participants felt that as the world's largest supplier of direct capital, the United States was in a very good position to be the leader in adopting responsible taxation. The United States has encouraged the Organization for Economic Cooperation and Development to investigate the tax-haven problems. Some foreign governments have already begun studying the U. S. law, and in particular the accounting problems involved in the definition of the earnings and profits of foreign corporations. The ultimate solution may result from international conferences and the adoption of common codes of behavior, possibly overseen by the United Nations, but until then the United States must legislate as it sees fit.

The administration's proposal to subsidize foreign investment in less developed countries through a 30 percent tax credit was also discussed. Many criticisms of the proposal were presented. The proposal might encourage the hostility of foreign local businessmen in the less developed countries that must compete against heavily subsidized American subsidiaries—although this view was disputed by some participants. Also, American domestic producers would be subject to unfair competition from imports coming from foreign subsidiaries of American firms that had gained this subsidy. The United States might well be subjected to the charge of economic imperialism since the subsidy does not distinguish between countries desiring foreign private investment and those less friendly to it. Since the proposal differentiates between types of investment, and denies the subsidy for some purposes, the subsidy would lead to a misallocation of capital and might be inefficient in general. The subsidy might also induce foreigners to establish U. S. corporations to invest abroad and thus the U. S. government would provide part of the cost of an investment that would have been made anyway.

Conclusion

The taxation of foreign-source income in the future will neither be static, nor will it likely become noncontroversial. International business is evolving rapidly, and the ways of doing business are constantly changing. The internationalization of business in the next twenty-five years will pose many challenges to tax law and tax administration. Tax equity in this field is extremely important, but the response of the United States to these challenges will be determined not only by equity principles, but also by its general attitude toward foreign investment. Today the United States encourages private investment in less developed countries primarily for raising living standards in these countries, as well as for the political benefit that might be derived by having economic development stimulated in those areas, particularly by private enterprise. The United States also favors American investment in developed areas because of the economic gains of high profits and the access to foreign technology. The United States may also benefit politically from having American firms share in the economies of the developed countries. All of these considerations will have to be weighed as the United States attempts to evolve an enlightened and efficient policy for the future.

List of Conference Participants

Robert Z. Aliber
  Agency for International Development

Robert Anthoine
  Columbia University Law School

Roy Blough
  Columbia University

Walter Blum
  University of Chicago Law School

Robert D. Calkins
  The Brookings Institution

John Costelloe
  Chabborn, Park, Whiteside and Wolff

Kenneth Dam
  University of Chicago Law School

Charles Davis
  Hopkins, Sutter, Owen, Mulroy & Wentz

Emanuel Demos
  Harvard Law School

Richard Goode
  The Brookings Institution

Nathan Gordon
  U. S. Treasury Department

Henry Gumpel
  Price Waterhouse & Company

Thomas Jenks
  Lee, Toomey and Kent

Lawrence Krause
  The Brookings Institution

Hal Lary
  National Bureau of Economic Research

James Mahon
  Lybrand, Ross Bros. and Montgomery

Leslie Mills
  Price Waterhouse & Company

Oliver Oldman
  Harvard Law School

Elizabeth Owens
  Harvard Law School

William Patty
  Sherman and Sterling

Joseph A. Pechman
  The Brookings Institution

Fred Peel
  Alvord and Alvord

Clifford Porter
  Cahill, Gordon, Reindel, and Ohl

Leo Raskind
  Vanderbilt University Law School

Peggy Musgrave
  University of Pennsylvania

Sidney Roberts
Roberts and Holland

Stanford Ross
New York University

Walter S. Salant
The Brookings Institution

Dan Throop Smith
Harvard University

Stanley S. Surrey
U. S. Treasury Department

David R. Tillinghast
U. S. Treasury Department

Ira Wender
Baker, MacKenzie and Hightower

Lawrence Woodworth
Joint Committee on Internal Revenue

Appendixes

APPENDIX A

Taxation of Foreign Income: Constitutional and International Law Aspects[1]

SOME LAWYERS HAVE ARGUED publicly that the elimination of deferral by imposing a tax on the shareholder would be unconstitutional. Therefore, it seems desirable that a portion of this background study be devoted to that topic. I am of the opinion that there is no substantial constitutional objection to such a tax with respect to foreign-source income of U. S. controlled foreign corporations. Because space is necessarily limited, and this study will not be published for lawyers alone, it is not possible to make an exhaustive analysis of all the issues involved, some of which raise quite subtle questions concerning the taxing power. Nevertheless, the main outline of the conflicting arguments can be stated.[2]

As a matter of principle, there would appear to be three possible bases of invalidity: First, the tax violates the due process clause of the Fifth Amendment. Second, the tax is not a tax on "income" under the Sixteenth Amendment and therefore, as a direct tax, is invalid because it is not apportioned among the states according to population. And, third, while not strictly speaking unconstitutional, the tax is a violation of public international law which, under general principles, is a part of U. S. domestic law.

[1] By Kenneth W. Dam.

[2] For arguments that a tax on the shareholders of a foreign corporation would be unconstitutional, see the opinion letter of Colin F. Stam, Chief of Staff of the Joint Committee on Internal Revenue Taxation dated May 4, 1961, in *President's 1961 Tax Recommendations*, Hearings before the House Committee on Ways and Means, 87 Cong. 1 sess. (1961), Vol. 1, p. 311, and the testimony and a statement of Adrian A. Kagen testifying against H.R. 10650 in *Revenue Act of 1962*, Hearings before the Senate Committee on Finance, 87 Cong. 2 sess. (1962) Pt. 7, p. 3042.

107

The due process argument would have to be founded on the proposition that the United States has no jurisdiction to tax the foreign-source income of foreign corporations, even though the taxation is limited to the proportion of such income represented by U. S. stock ownership. While there might be some merit to that contention, particularly where the foreign corporation has no business contacts with the United States,[3] imposing the tax on the U. S. shareholder instead of the foreign corporation would appear to change somewhat the nature of the problem. Such a tax on the shareholder is hard to distinguish from the foreign personal holding company provisions sustained in *Eder v. Commissioner*, 138 F.2d 27 (2nd Cir. 1943). Under those provisions, a U. S. shareholder of a foreign corporation which meets certain gross income and stock ownership requirements must include in gross income his aliquot portion of the "undistributed foreign personal holding company income" of the foreign corporation. In upholding the constitutionality of this tax, a distinguished panel of the Second Circuit (with Jerome Frank writing an opinion concurred in by Learned and Augustus Hand) found no substantial constitutional question. The only constitutional problem they thought worth discussing arose from blocking the Colombian pesos earned by the Colombian corporation. The taxpayer argued that "inability to expend income in the United States, or to use any portion of it in paying income taxes, necessarily precludes taxability."[4] The court dismissed that contention rather summarily, observing that "in a variety of circumstances it has been held that the fact that the distribution of income is prevented by operation of law, or by agreement among private parties, is no bar to its taxability" (138 F. 2d 28). It concluded that since the purpose of Congress—to deal with "incorporated pocketbooks" seeking to avoid U. S. taxes through use of foreign holding companies—was permissible and that the method chosen—imposing the tax on the shareholder—was a reasonable means to achieve that purpose, the tax was con-

[3] The Supreme Court has not yet ruled on the permissible geographical reach of the federal taxing power. It has held, however, that, in the case of state taxation, there must be "some definite link, some minimum connection, between a state and the person, property or transaction it seeks to tax." *Miller Bros. Co. v. Maryland*, 347 U. S. 340, 344–345 (1954); see *Scripto v. Carson*, 362 U. S. 207, 210–211 (1960). The special role of the Supreme Court in rationalizing the conflicting claims of the various states doubtless leads the court to a more stringent view of the taxing power of the states than it would take when the conflicting claims are advanced by the federal government and foreign governments.

[4] 138 F. 2d 28. It should be noted that the 1962 legislation provides that in computing the minimum distribution, the U. S. shareholder may exclude any income where it is established to the satisfaction of the Treasury that such income has been blocked by currency or other restrictions. Sec. 963 (c) (4) (A).

stitutional. Thus, in the light of the *Eder* case, even if Congress should go so far as to decide that all deferral constitutes a form of tax avoidance and should seek to prevent such avoidance by a tax on the U. S. shareholder, it would be rash to argue that the tax would be unconstitutional, however unwise one might consider the congressional action.[5] This conclusion is even more compelling in the case of tax haven and unreasonable accumulations legislation.

The second constitutional argument against elimination of deferral rests on the dual proposition that a tax on the U. S. shareholder measured by that shareholder's aliquot portion of the undistributed earnings of an American controlled foreign corporation would not be a tax on "income" within the meaning of the Sixteenth Amendment, and further that such a tax is a "direct tax" not apportioned among the states according to population.[6]

One might concede that if the tax on the shareholder is not a tax on income, it would be a direct tax under *Pollock v. Farmer's Loan & Trust Co.*, 157 U. S. 429, 158 U. S. 601 (1895), the decision which invalidated a 2 percent corporate income tax thereby leading to the passage of the Sixteenth Amendment. But it is highly questionable whether the fact that the shareholder, rather than the foreign corporation, is taxed makes the tax any less a tax on income. To be sure, in *Eisner v. Macomber*, 252 U. S. 189,

[5] It might be argued that the statute would be inapplicable where a U. S. shareholder holds less than a controlling interest and would be unable to force a dividend. The same argument, however, could be made with respect to the foreign personal holding company tax because a U. S. shareholder of such a holding company is taxed, however minute his interest may be. It is to be noted that, as in the case of the 1962 legislation, the foreign personal holding company provisions become operative only when the total stock interest of all U. S. citizens or residents exceeds 50 percent of the outstanding stock at some point during the taxable year. Thus, although no single U. S. shareholder has the power to force dividends, the U. S. shareholders as a group have that power. Except in unusual cases where several classes of voting stock having different dividend or liquidation rights are involved, the U. S. group will not have divergent interests with respect to declaration of dividends, at least so far as corporate policy is concerned (though they may sometimes have conflicting personal interests concerning dividends because of different personal tax brackets, credit ratings, etc.). The statute would therefore not be unconstitutional on its face. Further, it seems unlikely, in view of this normal identity of interest, that the tax would be held unconstitutional as applied where the shareholders' interests conflicted.

[6] The Sixteenth Amendment provides: "The Congress shall have power to lay and collect taxes on incomes, from whatever source derived, without apportionment among the several States, and without regard to any census or enumeration." The apportionment requirement with respect to direct taxes is found in Article I, Section 9, Clause 4: "No Capitation, or other direct, Tax shall be laid, unless in proportion to the Census or Enumeration herein before directed to be taken."

219 (1920), the Supreme Court, in the process of holding that Congress had no power to tax a common stock dividend issued to holders of common stock, rejected the government contention that Congress had "the power to levy a tax on the stockholder's share in accumulated profits of the corporation even before division by the declaration of a dividend of any kind." The court emphasized that "what is called the stockholder's share in the accumulated profits of the company is capital, not income," and that "a stockholder has no individual share in the accumulated profits, or in any particular part of the assets of the corporation, prior to dividend declared."

The force of this dictum, which was hardly necessary to the court's holding that a dividend of common on common gives rise to no income, was undercut by the powerful dissenting opinion of Justice Brandeis (as well as a one-paragraph dissent by Justice Holmes). Moreover, the dictum in the *Eisner* case has been seriously discredited by later decisions. For example, in *Helvering v. National Grocery Co.*, 304 U. S. 282 (1938) the Supreme Court stated that Congress could tax a sole shareholder on the profits of his corporation. And in a series of cases commencing in 1936, the Supreme Court severely limited *Eisner v. Macomber* by holding that a stock dividend is constitutionally taxable where the proportionate interest of the shareholder is altered.[7] The effect of those decisions was to undercut sharply the rationale of the *Eisner* case that shareholders may not be taxed on undistributed profits. While *Eisner v. Macomber* makes sense on its facts (that dividends of common on common are not taxed), it is doubtful that it today represents a constitutional doctrine.[8] In 1955, the Supreme Court made it rather clear, in two cases which unfortunately did not squarely raise the issue, that *Eisner v. Macomber* was not to be interpreted as announcing a constitutional principle but, rather, simply a judge-made, subconstitutional rule relating to realization of income in stock dividend cases.[9] Thus, the 1871 case of *Collector v. Hubbard*, 12 Wall. 1 (1871), which sustained a Civil War tax on a shareholder with respect to undistributed profits, is probably the constitutional rule today, even though that case was said in the *Eisner v. Macomber* opinion to have been overruled by *Pol-*

---

[7] *Koshland v. Helvering*, 298 U. S. 441 (1936); cf. *Helvering v. Griffiths*, 318 U. S. 371 (1943); *Helvering v. Sprouse*, 318 U. S. 604 (1943).

[8] In *Helvering v. Griffiths, op. cit.*, three dissenting Justices (Douglas, Black, and Murphy) called for the overruling of the *Eisner* case and the majority refused to pass on the point, though recognizing that "the question of the constitutional validity of *Eisner v. Macomber* is plainly one of the first magnitude" (318 U. S. at 394).

[9] *Commissioner v. Glenshaw Glass Co.*, 348 U. S. 426, 431 (1955); *General American Investors Co. v. Commissioner*, 348 U. S. 434 (1955).

lock v. Farmer's Loan & Trust Co. This conclusion is forcefully supported by the 1943 decision in *Eder v. Commissioner,* which did not even deign to consider the *Eisner v. Macomber* dictum in sustaining the constitutionality of the foreign personal holding company tax.

The international law argument against a tax on the shareholder is based on the theory, difficult to establish from international law sources, that no country has the power to tax the foreign-source income of aliens. A foreign corporation is assumed for this purpose to be an alien. This argument loses whatever force it might be thought to possess when the tax is imposed on the U. S. shareholder, whether a domestic corporation or a U. S. citizen. It is axiomatic that in the absence of treaty, public international law gives an individual no rights against his national state. Even if the tax were imposed on the foreign corporation, the international law argument is of questionable validity where the foreign corporation is managed from the United States, as in the case of many foreign subsidiaries of U. S. corporations. Lawyers trained in the United States are likely to overlook the fact that in many other countries tests such as the place of management and control or the locus of the administration are used to determine nationality. In view of these diverse practices, the place of incorporation can hardly be elevated to the status of the sole international law test of nationality for all purposes.

APPENDIX B

Taxation of Foreign-Source Income by Other Countries[1]

A COMPREHENSIVE STUDY of the taxation of foreign-source income in all countries other than the United States would require more space than is available for this background study. Thus, Appendix B is limited to the basic principles of taxation of foreign-source corporate income by ten representative countries—Belgium, Canada, the Federal Republic of Germany, France, Italy, Japan, the Netherlands, Sweden, Switzerland, and the United Kingdom.

An exhaustive description of the rules applying to foreign-source income taxation even for these countries would require an analysis of the tax system as a whole. And a comprehensive study would have to include the pertinent provisions of the more than 150 international tax treaties that the countries surveyed have concluded among themselves and with other nations. Furthermore, it would have to extend to the international aspects of the major "indirect" taxes such as turnover, excise, and sales taxes—which are more important than income taxes as a source of government revenue in some of the countries surveyed—as well as of the taxes on property or net worth. Instead of such a detailed analysis, this study summarizes similarities and differences in the treatment of foreign-source income in the ten countries as a means of highlighting some of the problems involved in devising tax policies in the United States.

Most countries tax corporations which are considered to be residents of their territory on foreign-source as well as domestic income, and limit the taxation of nonresidents to income from sources in their territory. Within this general framework, the jurisdictional principles vary from country to country. No two countries agree on the definition of the term "residence" as applied to individuals, corporations, and other taxable entities or associ-

---

[1] By Leslie Mills and Henry J. Gumpel.

112

ations.[2] Corporate tax residence may be defined in terms of the place of incorporation, the place of effective management and control, the place where the principal business establishment is located, or any combination of these factors. Some countries—including France, Japan, and the United Kingdom—distinguish between various degrees of residence in order to ensure, or prevent, the taxation of certain income to certain classes of individual taxpayers. Since tax residence, in any country, is a basic condition for asserting jurisdiction over foreign income, the first part of the appendix summarizes the rules that determine the residence for tax purposes of corporations in the countries surveyed.

Even more conflicting than the various national rules on corporate tax residence are those that determine whether the source of income is domestic or foreign. The diversities in this area are multiplied under the schedular systems of income taxation prevalent in Europe and other parts of the world. The systems classify income in different categories, according to the nature of the income-producing activity, and often establish different rules on sources of income for the different categories of income. While the source rules of a particular country are primarily important for nonresidents who are taxed only on income earned inside that country, they also are of considerable interest to resident taxpayers with income from sources outside the country. Although residents are generally taxed on a world-wide basis, all capital-exporting countries provide, in one form or another, for special treatment of foreign income—either as an incentive for foreign investment or in order to equalize the tax treatment of domestic and foreign income. The source rules of the various countries and those on the tax treatment of foreign income are discussed in the parts of this appendix which deal with the various types of income.

Prior to the advent of more modern systems of income taxation, many countries adopted the principle of the territoriality of taxation, according to which only income from sources in the particular country is subject to its tax jurisdiction. Important residues of this principle still exist in the Latin countries where it was first applied. The specific rules are discussed later in connection with the various classifications of foreign income.

Although a detailed description of the various national income tax systems is outside the scope of this study, a brief reference should be made to the wide differences which exist among these systems in the method of

---

[2] For the sake of simplicity, the term "corporation," as used here, includes not only corporations in the proper sense, but also other entities with independent legal existence, such as the limited liability company and the partnership limited by shares, which are found in the civil law countries. In general, these entities are treated like corporations for tax purposes.

computing taxable income from domestic or foreign sources. As an example, most European countries—as well as Japan—determine taxable income from "business" (and sometimes from "other activities") according to the method of net worth comparison, and taxable income from "other sources" as the excess of gross income over related expenses. When the method of net worth comparison applies, taxable income is computed as the increase in the taxpayer's net worth from the beginning to the end of the taxable year, with certain adjustments for tax purposes. Under this method, the valuation of assets and liabilities at the relevant points of time has a direct and decisive effect on the determination of taxable income. In view of the existing diversities in computing the tax base, a mere comparison of tax rates is almost meaningless, and rates are mentioned in this appendix only to illustrate the application of certain principles of taxation.

Methods of Avoiding Double Taxation

The rules of taxation discussed in this survey are those of the local law of the various countries. To a greater or lesser extent, these rules are modified by international treaties for the avoidance or mitigation of double taxation. In the main, the treaties accomplish this result by applying one of two methods:

Under the "exclusion" or "exemption" method which is generally followed in the intra-European treaties, the contracting countries divide the various objects of taxation among themselves, and the country which renounces its right to tax certain income under a treaty will not exercise this right, even though the other country may not tax the income in a specific case.[3] However, in order to prevent a taxpayer from securing the benefit of reduced income tax rates both at his domicile and in the source country, the country of domicile usually reserves the right to consider the excluded portion of the income in computing its tax on the portion of the income that is not exempt.[4]

The other method of preventing double taxation, applied in the Anglo-American countries and Japan, is the foreign tax credit. Unlike the exclusion method, the foreign tax credit prevents only actual, and not potential,

[3] As a singular exception to this otherwise universal rule, article 3(3) of the French Tax Reform Law of December 28, 1959, states that French individual or corporate income tax shall apply to all income which is assigned to France by a tax treaty, any conflicting rule of French tax law notwithstanding.

[4] This qualified exemption method is termed "exclusion with progression" in the reports of the Fiscal Committee of the Organization for Economic Cooperation and Development. It is of practical significance to those corporations or other entities taxed at graduated rates under the local law.

double taxation. And it is less favorable to the taxpayer if the effective tax rate in the country of source is lower than that in the country of domicile. In the tax treaties between countries of Continental Europe and Anglo-American countries, the former usually apply the exclusion method, and the latter the credit method for preventing the double taxation of income which has its source in the other contracting country.

Regardless of the method applied, the essential feature of every tax treaty is the imposition of restrictions on the taxing power of either the country of domicile or the country of source. Whether the contracting countries will accept such restrictions, and the extent to which they will accept them, depends to a large degree on their relative position as debtor or creditor nations. For this reason, tax treaties between the industrialized countries, on the one hand, and between such countries and less developed nations, on the other, contain important differences. In addition, the intensity of the taxpayer's connection with the source country will determine the degree to which the source country is prepared to limit its tax jurisdiction.

In general, the source country will retain its taxing power on: (1) income from real property which is situated in its territory; (2) business income derived through a permanent establishment located there;[5] or (3) income from services which are performed in its area, either for a certain period of time or from a "fixed base." Conversely, the source country usually is prepared to limit its right to tax income from capital such as dividends, interest, or royalties, retaining for itself only a limited withholding tax on such income. This pattern is followed in all treaties concluded by the countries included in this survey, and only the details of the arrangements vary from one treaty to the other.

Rules on Tax Residence

For tax purposes, the rules concerning the residence of a corporation fall roughly into three general classes in the ten countries with which we are concerned here:

1. The residence is determined by the place of incorporation in Switzerland, Italy, Sweden, and Japan.

2. The residence is determined by the place of central control and management in the United Kingdom and France.

3. The residence is determined by either or both alternatives (1) and

---

[5] The taxation of shipping and aircraft corporations is usually assigned to the domicile of the corporation.

(2) above, and occasionally by other factors, in Canada, the Federal Republic of Germany, the Netherlands, and Belgium.

Under Swiss law, the "seat" (statutory office) of a corporation is located in the place where the corporation is listed in the Commercial Register. Substantially the same rule applies in Italy and Sweden.[6] Factors other than the place of organization, such as the location of management or of the corporate activities, are not material in these countries as far as corporate tax residence is concerned. The same jurisdictional rule applies in Japan, although the Corporation Tax Law of that country appears to indicate otherwise.

According to the Japanese law, a corporation will be treated as a resident of Japan if its head office or principal office is located in Japan. The head office or principal office is at the place formally designated as such in the articles of incorporation. As a matter of Japanese law, however, every corporation formed under Japanese law must designate a place in Japan as the location of its head office. Conversely, a corporation formed under the law of another country will not be considered a resident of Japan, although its principal business office or seat of management may be located there. Thus, for all practical purposes, Japanese tax jurisdiction is based on the place of incorporation.

For British tax purposes, a company is deemed to be resident at the place where its "central control and management actually abide."[7] Since factual control and management of a corporation can be exercised in more than one country, the seat of management, for practical purposes, is considered to be at the place where the directors' meetings are held, although other factors bearing on control may be considered in appropriate cases.

Basically the same rule applies in France. The location of the head office of the corporation (*siège social*) determines whether the corporation will be classified as a resident or nonresident of France. Under French corporation law, the charter of a corporation that is formed in France must designate a place in France as the location of the head office. In general, the office which is so designated will be considered the head office of the corporation for tax purposes. But if the facts indicate that the actual management of the corporation is conducted from a place outside France so that the charter office is "fictitious," the place where actual management occurs determines the status of the corporation as a resident or nonresident.

Canada follows the British rule and treats a corporation as resident if its central management and control are exercised in Canada. As under

---

[6] An exception of limited importance applies in the case of holding companies formed under the law of a foreign country which are owned by Swedish residents and managed and controlled in Sweden.

[7] *De Beers Consol. Mines, Ltd. v. Howe* (1906), 5 T. C. 198 (H.L.).

British law, the seat of effective management is primarily determined by the place at which the directors of the company meet. However, a recent (1961) amendment to the Income Tax Law introduced incorporation in Canada as an alternative factor through which corporate tax residence will be established, provided that the corporation also carries on business in Canada at any time during the taxable year.

Under the tax law of the Federal Republic of Germany, a corporation is treated as resident if either its seat or its place of management is located in West Germany. "Seat" is a legal concept and denotes the place at which the corporation is listed in the Commercial Register maintained at the local court. "Place of management" is defined as the place where the important business decisions are made. This place is usually, although not necessarily, the location at which the statutory representatives of the corporation exercise their functions. In extreme cases, however, it may be the domicile, the customary place of abode, or the place of management of the dominant individual or corporate shareholder. Substantially the same rules are followed in the Netherlands.

Belgium applies a threefold definition of corporate tax residence. A corporation will be deemed to be resident in Belgium if its statutory office, or the place of effective management, or the principal business establishment is located in Belgium.

The rules of resident countries vary on the tax treatment of profits (or losses) which enterprises realize from direct business operations conducted outside the parent country. But there are a number of rules common to most, or all, of the ten countries we are studying.

Tax benefits, such as accelerated depreciation, reduced tax rates for distributed profits, or complete or partial exemption from tax for certain periods, are usually reserved for corporations organized under the laws of the country extending such benefits. Therefore, direct foreign operations through an unincorporated branch are less usual than those conducted through a foreign subsidiary, except during the initial stage of a foreign venture.

Rules on Taxation of Foreign-Source Income

All ten foreign countries under review here—like the United States—respect the separate identity of a foreign corporation, even though it is wholly owned by a domestic enterprise. None attempts to tax the profits of the foreign subsidiary until such profits are distributed to the parent. Exceptions to this deferral rule, which are more apparent than real, are found in those countries in which the situs of management and control of a corporation (as distinguished from the place of incorporation) furnishes the jurisdictional basis of resident taxation. The avoidance of the taxation of a subsidiary's profits by both the country of residence and the country of operations is one of the foremost objectives of international tax treaties. Without exception, the treaties of the countries being discussed assign the taxation of business profits that are realized through a "permanent establishment" to the country of operations, and impose restrictions on the taxing power of the country of residence—either by excluding such profits from the tax base, or by applying the foreign tax credit.

The following discussion concerns the determination of foreign business profits and the devices for avoiding or mitigating the double taxation of such profits which the various resident countries apply unilaterally—that is, in the absence of a tax treaty with the country of operations. Almost all countries apply such devices. These may take the form of a complete or partial exemption of foreign business profits, reduced tax rates on such profits, or a credit or deduction for the income taxes paid in the country of operation.

Exemption of Foreign Business Profits

Among the countries surveyed, France, Italy, Switzerland, and the Netherlands provide for tax exemption on the business profits of resident corporations from foreign sources under certain conditions. In France and Italy, the exemption of certain foreign business profits is predicated on the ancient principle of the territorial nature of income taxation. It may be noted in passing that this principle has been eroded so much that considerations of practical tax policy would seem to furnish a more convincing rationale for the rules enunciated in its name.

A French corporation is subject to income tax on profits realized through operations conducted in France, including the overseas departments of Guadeloupe, Guyana, Martinique, and Reunion. Profits from a permanent establishment (as defined under French law) located in another country are not subject to the corporation profits tax, provided that separate books are maintained for the establishment. Even in the absence of a foreign permanent establishment, profits from business activities conducted abroad are not taxable if such activities constitute a "complete cycle of operations" (*cycle commercial complet*), such as the purchase and sale of the same merchandise outside France. When foreign profits are not taxed, losses sustained in foreign operations cannot be offset against profits that are taxable in France.[8] The exemptions can be claimed only by the

---

[8] As an exception, the Decree of November 2, 1954, permitted French corporations to reduce their profits from French sources by losses incurred by foreign sales offices

French corporation and do not extend to the shareholder who receives a distribution from exempt profits.

In Italy, the principle of the territoriality of taxation applies to some of the taxes levied on business profits but not to others. Briefly stated, the Italian system of income taxation provides for a number of schedular taxes on various types or classifications of income. Among these, the tax on income from movable property (*imposta sui redditi di ricchezza mobile*) covers business income. These schedular taxes are supplemented by a complementary tax on individuals and a corporation tax (*imposta sulle societa*), somewhat like an excess profits tax. The latter tax applies both to the profits of the corporation and its net worth when profits exceed 6 percent of the book capital.

In the case of resident corporations, the schedular tax (*ricchezza mobile* tax) applies only to business profits realized in Italy. Foreign business profits are not subject to that tax, provided they are realized in a foreign permanent establishment for which separate books are maintained. To this extent, the Italian rule is similar to the one applied in France. It differs, however, since profits of the foreign permanent establishment which are exempted from foreign income tax under the rules of a tax treaty (such as profits from the operation of Italian ships or aircraft) become again taxable in Italy. Losses sustained in foreign business operations cannot be used as a credit against income that is taxable in Italy, if profits from the same source would be exempt from Italian tax under the rules discussed.

The rule of territoriality does not apply to the complementary tax on individuals, or the corporation tax. These taxes are therefore levied on foreign business income, as computed for determining the exemption from the *ricchezza mobile* tax, except that the complementary tax on individuals is limited to such foreign income as is remitted to Italy. Expenditures in connection with foreign business income are deductible, including foreign taxes on such income. The comparatively insignificant deduction of foreign income taxes is thus the only method for mitigating the double taxation of foreign business profits as far as the two supplementary taxes on business profits are concerned. More effective devices such as the foreign tax credit are considered unnecessary on the ground that the rule of territoriality precludes double taxation for purposes of the much more burdensome schedular tax.

Switzerland and the Netherlands have developed similar rules for exempting certain foreign business profits. In effect, the applicable provisions of the Swiss Federal Income Tax (Defense Tax) Law project the

and market research facilities for the first three years after the organization of such offices or facilities.

principles developed in the field of Swiss intercantonal taxation into the international sphere.[9] In general, business income which a resident of Switzerland (individual, partnership, or corporation) derives from a foreign permanent establishment is not subject to Swiss income tax. However, such profits are taken into consideration in computing the graduated individual income tax on the taxpayer's nonexempt income. Where separate books are maintained for the foreign permanent establishment, the exemption may be computed on that basis. Otherwise, the tax on total (domestic and foreign) income is reduced in the proportion which the "factors" pertaining to the foreign establishment bear to the factors pertaining to the enterprise as a whole.

The "factors" selected vary with the nature of the business concerned, such as capital employed and payroll in the case of manufacturing enterprises, the turnover of the business in the case of traders, or premium receipts in the case of insurance companies. However, the relevant elements are not prescribed by statute and the authorities may apply different criteria or combinations thereof in appropriate cases to determine the relative importance of the foreign establishment as a part of the entire enterprise. A special feature of Swiss federal income tax law is that a portion of the profits of a foreign business establishment can be allocated for taxation purposes to the Swiss head office of the enterprise on the ground that the management and supervision exercised by the head office contribute to the realization of profits by the establishment. This portion (called *praecipuum*) is determined as a percentage of the profits of the establishment (usually between 10 percent and 25 percent). Some of the tax treaties concluded by Switzerland preclude the application of this rule.

Unilateral exemptions for profits derived from foreign permanent establishments also apply in the Netherlands. Resident Dutch individuals or corporations can claim the exemption, provided that the foreign income is subject to a foreign tax whose structure is substantially similar to that of the Dutch individual or corporate income tax, and that the double taxation of the foreign income is not precluded either through other unilateral relief measures or the rules of an international tax treaty. The computation of the Dutch tax is most easily illustrated for individual taxpayers.

---

[9] While the Swiss Federal Constitution prohibits intercantonal double taxation in general terms, the specific application of this principle has never been defined by statute. As a result, the task of defining detailed rules fell to the Swiss Federal Court whose decisions in this area go back to the 1870's. While the cantonal rules on taxing foreign business profits are for the most part identical, or very similar, to the federal rules, no attempt can be made in this study to present the detailed legal provisions applying in the 25 cantons.

The reduction of the individual tax is computed in the ratio of qualifying foreign income to total taxable income, as indicated below:

Taxable income from Netherlands sources......................Fl.	10,000
Taxable income from foreign sources..........................	5,000
Total taxable income....................................Fl.	15,000
Tax on Fl. 15,000, from tax table...........................Fl.	4,980
Reduction: $\dfrac{5{,}000}{15{,}000}\times 4{,}980$..................................	−1,660
Tax payable..Fl.	3,320

The reduction of Dutch income tax is thus not dependent on the rate of the foreign tax. Where the effective rate of the foreign tax is lower than that of the graduated Dutch individual income tax, this method is more beneficial to the taxpayer than a credit for foreign taxes would be.

Although the same rules apply to the foreign income of resident Dutch corporations, the recent introduction of a proportionate corporate tax rate (45 percent) virtually exempts the foreign profits from Dutch corporate tax. Losses sustained in foreign operations can be offset against profits from such operations during the six-year carry-over period generally provided by Dutch law. They cannot, however, be used as a credit against business profits from Dutch sources.

Reduction of Tax Rates

The ten countries use various methods for reducing the corporate tax rates on foreign-source income. For example, Swedish corporations may deduct reinvested foreign income; the United Kingdom, Canada, and Japan receive credit for income taxes paid to the country of operations; some British companies can qualify as British Overseas Trade Corporations (O.T.C.) and can take specified exemptions; and so on. Even Belgium provides certain benefits, although it does not distinguish between the business income derived from domestic and foreign sources in determining the tax base for purposes of corporate income taxes. Belgian corporations pay only one-fourth of the regular tax on profits derived from branches or other business establishments maintained abroad.[10] Apparently, this tax

[10] Under the new Belgian Income Tax Law introduced by the Reform Law of November 20, 1962, the standard rate of the corporate income tax is 30 percent. Undistributed profits in excess of B. fr. 5,000,000 (U. S. $100,000) are taxed at the rate of 35 percent; however, the additional 5 percent tax on that portion of income is refunded

benefit is not available to resident individuals receiving income from direct business operations abroad.

DEDUCTION FOR REINVESTED FOREIGN INCOME. Sweden taxes Swedish corporations on the entire amount of their income from domestic or foreign sources, and relies on its system of international tax treaties to prevent the double taxation of income or profits from foreign sources. There are no unilateral relief measures that would apply in the absence of a treaty with the country of source, with one comparatively insignificant, but interesting, exception. A Swedish corporation can arrange to conduct its foreign operations as an "independent business," which requires that the foreign operations be strictly separated from the business activities conducted in Sweden. In the language of the Swedish tax statutes, the foreign operations must be "entirely different" from those operating in Sweden and have no "inner connection" with the latter. Under these conditions, the portion of the foreign profits that is reinvested abroad is deductible in computing taxable income. In effect, a limited tax deferral is granted when foreign income is reinvested in the foreign business.

FOREIGN INCOME TAX CREDIT. While residents of the United Kingdom, Canada, and Japan are subject to taxation at the full rates on foreign as well as domestic business income, they are entitled to a credit for taxes paid on such income to the country of operations.

The British foreign tax credit was introduced at about the same time as the U. S. foreign tax credit, and originally was limited to taxes imposed by the dominions and colonies. In some respects, it is more liberal than the corresponding credits granted under the laws of the United States, the Federal Republic of Germany, and Japan. In others it is less liberal; British tax law does not provide for a carry-over or carry-back of unused foreign tax credits or for an overall limitation on the credit. It is not required that income from foreign sources be recomputed according to U.K. rules for purposes of the credit, as long as the income which has borne foreign tax is the same as the income taxed in the United Kingdom. Also, the taxable periods need not be the same under U.K. rules and those of the foreign country that imposes the creditable tax. Consequently, foreign tax credit is not necessarily lost as a result of the fact that the rules of the foreign jurisdiction differ from the British rules with respect to principles of tax accounting, deductions, exemptions, exclusions, or tax-

---

if the profits are distributed. The effective tax rate on foreign profits is thus 7.5 or 8.75 percent. The new corporate income tax became effective January 1, 1963.

able periods, although the effective rate of the British tax—and thus the amount of the available credit—in some cases may be reduced through deductions or exclusions from income (such as capital gains) that are available in the United Kingdom but not in the foreign country.

British tax law also permits the current offset of foreign branch losses against domestic income, and a carry-forward of such losses to future taxable years without time limitation. If the effective rate of the foreign tax exceeds that of the British tax on the same income, the portion of the foreign tax which cannot be credited can be deducted from taxable foreign income.

A resident British corporation—a company managed and controlled in the United Kingdom—is, in general, subject to both standard tax (presently at the rate of 38.75 percent) and profits tax (presently at the rate of 15 percent) even though all of its operations are conducted abroad and all of its income is derived from foreign sources. An important exception to this rule applies to British companies that qualify as Overseas Trade Corporations (O.T.C.).[11] An O.T.C. is a resident British company whose trade is wholly carried on abroad.[12] To qualify as an O.T.C., the company must avoid any dealings in the United Kingdom which, if conducted by a nonresident, would be considered as trading in that country. Certain permissible activities in the United Kingdom, and others that are not permissible, are defined in the statute. In addition, an O.T.C. must operate abroad in a manner that will subject it to the income tax of the country or countries of operations, or which would subject it to income tax if the foreign country were to impose such a tax.

An O.T.C. is exempt from United Kingdom standard tax and profits tax on its trading income, but subject to both these taxes with respect to investment income. The exemption of trading profits from standard tax ends when these profits are distributed as a dividend, or when the company is liquidated or loses its O.T.C. status and ceases to trade. An O.T.C. that distributes a dividend is permittted to deduct standard tax from the distribution in the usual manner; the recipient of the dividend includes the grossed-up amount of the distribution in income, and claims credit for the standard tax paid, as in the case of other dividends. The only tax that is levied on trading profits of an O.T.C. occurs when a distribution of such profits is put into the hands of a corporate shareholder which is subject to the profits tax.

[11] The O.T.C. rules were introduced by the Finance Act of 1957.

[12] In addition, a resident holding company that owns more than a 50 percent interest in an O.T.C. and does not own shares in any subsidiary that trades in the United Kingdom qualifies as an O.T.C.

The Canadian rules on the taxation of income from direct foreign business operations are substantially similar to those of the United Kingdom. Resident Canadian corporations are required to include the foreign income in the tax base and are permitted to credit the foreign tax on that income against the Canadian tax. Income that is taxable in the foreign country but not in Canada, such as foreign capital gains, is not included in the base of the Canadian tax, and foreign taxes paid on such income do not qualify for the foreign tax credit. Unlike the U.K. rule, the Canadian rule does not permit an excess amount of a foreign creditable tax to be claimed as a deduction from income.

A corporation whose head office or main office is located in Japan in general is taxed on its world-wide income. However, a Japanese corporation's income from export transactions is granted special tax treatment. Its taxable income from such transactions may be reduced by varying percentages (between 1 percent and 5 percent) of gross export income, up to a maximum of 80 percent of taxable export income. A similar rule applies to income from the transmission of know-how abroad, subject to limitations of 50 percent of gross income or 50 percent of taxable income, whichever is less.

Apart from the special treatment of income from exports or the transmission of know-how, statutory relief from double taxation is accomplished by the foreign tax credit. The credit is limited to the lesser of the foreign tax or the Japanese tax on a per country or overall basis. There is no provision for a carry-back or carry-over of foreign tax in excess of the limitation. The credit cannot be claimed for the portion of a foreign tax attributable to income for which the deduction in connection with exports or the transmission of know-how abroad is allowable.

Alternative Forms of Relief

Among the countries discussed in this study, the Federal Republic of Germany appears to provide the greatest variety of devices for avoiding or mitigating international double taxation. Among the available methods— for which application to specific situations is minutely prescribed by statute—are the exclusion of foreign income from the tax base, the foreign tax credit, the taxation of certain foreign income at a flat rate, and tax deferral for certain investments in developing countries. Since the application of any one of these methods is limited to income from foreign sources, and the rules on the domestic or foreign sources of business income are different from those applying in other countries, a brief discussion of the rules applicable to source seems appropriate.

The general rule is that resident individuals and entities are taxable on a world-wide basis—that is, on foreign as well as domestic income. Within the schedular classification "business income," the law distinguishes between business income in the technical sense (profits from the operation of a business), and certain income or gains generally classified under one of the other categories of taxable income but are treated as business income if originating in the operation of a business. Examples of such income or gains include rentals, royalties, service income, dividends, interest and other income from capital, and gain from the sale of shares in a corporation or other commercial entity.

This distinction applies to business income from foreign sources as well as to domestic business income. Its practical importance, in the context discussed here, lies in the fact that business income in the technical sense (income from the operation of a business) is deemed to be from foreign sources only if it is realized in a foreign permanent establishment or through the activities of a permanent representative stationed abroad. In contrast, the characterization as foreign income of profits or gains that become business income through the operation of the attribution rules is not dependent on this requirement. Consequently, profits from export sales to a foreign country that are not realized through an establishment or representative located abroad are classified as domestic income and do not qualify for any form of relief that is available for foreign income. Conversely, income from the licensing of a patent in a foreign country, or gain from the sale of shares of a nonresident corporation, is classified as foreign income and qualifies for relief, although it is not connected with a foreign establishment or representative.

To the extent that income from foreign sources is withdrawn from German taxation under the rules of a tax treaty—for example, business income accruing in a permanent establishment in the other treaty country —the Federal Republic excludes such income from the tax base, with the usual reservation that it may consider the amount of the excluded income in computing the tax on the nonexempt income.

This method of "exclusion with progression" is applied only in international tax treaties and not as a unilateral device for avoiding double taxation. In the absence of a treaty with the country of source, the Federal Republic grants a foreign tax credit for national foreign income taxes imposed on the taxpayer. The credit is available on a per country basis, and limited in the proportion of foreign net income to total net income. There is, at present, no provision for an overall limitation for the carry-over or carry-back of unused foreign tax credits. A deduction from income is available only for foreign income taxes that are not creditable, such as those imposed by the political subdivisions of a foreign country. However, the foreign tax credit can also be claimed for foreign taxes on income from treaty countries if the treaty fails to prevent the double taxation of income. As far as this rule applies, the credit is available for foreign state or local taxes, provided that they are specifically named in the applicable treaty.

As an alternative to the foreign tax credit, the resident German taxpayer can elect to be taxed on certain income from nontreaty countries at a flat rate (the present rate is 25 percent, and its reduction is under consideration). This form of relief can be claimed for profits of foreign permanent establishments engaged in producing or selling merchandise abroad, rendering services abroad, or importing merchandise from the foreign country to West Germany. Compared to the foreign tax credit, flat rate taxation is beneficial where the rate of the foreign tax is low. In addition, it is apt to preserve the benefit of tax reductions or exemptions in the country of source. Taxation at the present flat rate of 25 percent can also be claimed for income from international transportation services.

Taxation of Dividends

The income tax laws of most countries include provisions designed to mitigate the double taxation of corporate profits which results if such profits are subjected to full taxation while held by the corporation that earned them, and again by the shareholder who receives them in the form of a dividend. Although the various relief provisions apply primarily to distributions made by domestic corporations, they are as a rule extended to foreign dividends, because of the detrimental effect that double taxation has on international business.

Avoidance or mitigation of double taxation at the corporate level is accomplished by applying reduced corporate income tax rates to that portion of a corporation's profits which is distributed as a dividend. This system is applied in the Federal Republic of Germany, which, with certain exceptions, taxes the distributed profits of corporations and other commercial entities at the rate of 15 percent and retained earnings at the rate of 51 percent. The introduction of a "split" corporate tax rate is under consideration in the Netherlands,[13] and its adoption by all member countries of the European Economic Community has been recommended by the "Report of the Fiscal Committee on Tax Harmonization in the

[13] However, the government bill provides for a differential of only 15 percent between the rates on distributed profits and on retained earnings, compared to a 36 percent rate differential in West Germany.

Common Market."[14] Since split corporate tax rates, where they exist, apply to distributions by resident corporations, regardless of the domestic or foreign origin of the income that is distributed, a detailed discussion of this method would not be pertinent to the present study.

Relief measures for the shareholder exist in very different forms. They may take the form of a complete or partial exclusion of dividend income from the recipient's tax base. This exclusion, in turn, may be unconditional (as in Canada); or it may be subject to limitations (as in Switzerland, the Netherlands, and West Germany) on the relative size of the shareholder's investment in the distributing corporation, the time during which the investment was held, or a combination of these and other factors. Under other systems, reduced tax rates apply to foreign dividend income either generally (as in France and Belgium) or at the shareholder's option (as in Italy and West Germany). Still other systems do not reduce the tax base or apply lower tax rates, but prevent the double taxation of foreign dividends through a more or less liberal foreign tax credit (as in the United Kingdom, Japan, Canada, and West Germany). Or the relief may be issued under provisions of tax treaties (as in Sweden).

Exemption of Intercorporate Dividends

If a Canadian corporation owns more than 25 percent of a foreign corporation, its dividends are excluded from the tax base of the recipient entity. The exclusion is not contingent on a minimum holding period.

Under the income tax laws of the Swiss confederation and those of a number of cantons, a Swiss corporation can claim a reduction of tax for dividends received from another (Swiss or foreign) corporation, provided that its investment amounts to not less than 20 percent of the latter's paid-in capital, or 2 million Swiss francs in value. The reduction of tax is computed in the ratio of qualifying dividend income to total gross income. It, therefore, does not amount to a full exemption on dividend income, except in the case of pure holding companies.

Under the tax law of the Netherlands, a resident Dutch corporation can claim full exemption for dividends that it receives from another (Dutch or foreign) corporation under the following conditions: In general, the investment must amount to not less than 25 percent of the paid-in share capital of the distributing corporation. However, holdings less than 25 percent will suffice if the Minister of Finance certifies that the invest-

---

[14] A translation of this report (usually referred to as the "Neumark Report") is included in the *Common Market Reporter* published by Commerce Clearing House, Inc. (1963).

ment is in the national interest.[15] In addition, there must be no mutual investments between the holding company and the corporation in which the investment is made. The foreign corporation must also be subject to a tax in the country of its domicile. This is substantially similar to the Netherlands corporate income tax.[16] Whether the dividends as such are subject to tax in the foreign country is immaterial for purposes of the exemption.

In this connection, the relevant tax law of the Federal Republic of Germany applies to dividends which a resident corporation receives from a foreign corporation that qualifies as a German resident, of which at least 25 percent is owned by the recipient of the dividend. Such dividends are exempt from corporation income tax and trade tax on business profits in the hands of the recipient entity on condition that the latter redistributes the dividend to its own shareholders.[17] This exemption (termed "holding privilege" or "affiliation privilege") does not apply to foreign dividends as a matter of German statutory law. It is, however, extended to distributions made by at least 25 percent-owned foreign corporations under the tax treaties concluded by the Federal Republic with the Netherlands, Luxembourg, Sweden, Norway, India, and the United Arab Republic (Egypt).

According to the interpretation placed by the German Federal Tax Administration on the treaties with the United States and the United Kingdom, dividends which an individual resident of Germany or a German corporation receives from a U. S. or British corporation are excluded from the tax base of the recipient, provided that such dividends are not exempt from tax in the other country.[18]

Partial Exclusion of Foreign Dividend Income

A resident French corporation holding a certain minimum of the issued capital of a French or foreign corporation is taxed only on a portion of the dividends distributed by such a corporation. The reduction of the tax base applies to investments which are held in the form of nominative

[15] As an exception, foreign dividends received by a Dutch investment company are not subject to the Netherlands corporation tax, whether the investment amounts to 25 percent or more, provided that the distributing corporation is subject to a foreign tax which is substantially similar to the Netherlands corporation tax.

[16] This requirement is interpreted liberally.

[17] If the recipient corporation does not redistribute the dividend, it becomes subject to a "supplementary tax," the rate of which is equal to the differential between the corporate tax rate on distributed profits and the rate on retained earnings (in general, 36 percent). The operating profits of the corporation receiving the dividend are deemed to be distributed first.

[18] The excluded dividend income is taken into account in computing the effective tax rate on the taxpayer's nonexempt income.

shares and which have been so held for at least two years, or from the inception of the distributing corporation.

The portions of the dividend included in taxable income are subjected to a corporation income tax at the rate of 50 percent. These taxable portions vary between 25 percent (if the investment in the issuing corporation amounts to 20 percent) and 5 percent (if the investment in the issuing corporation amounts to more than 50 percent). The computation of the taxable portions also varies according to the method of collecting the dividend. If collection is made through a French bank, the bank is required to withhold the French dividend tax, at the rate of 24 percent, from the amount collected (gross dividend less foreign withholding tax, if any). The taxable portion then is computed on the balance (76 percent) of the dividend received. No further dividend tax is payable if the recipient corporation redistributes the dividend to its own shareholders, provided that this redistribution is made in the year of receipt or the next following year.[19] In the event that the dividend is collected direct, the taxable portion is computed on the amount received, and withholding of dividend tax is required only if and when the recipient corporation redistributes the dividend to its own shareholders.[20]

The taxable portions of dividend income are arbitrary amounts that are deemed to approximate the (nondeductible) expenses incurred by the recipient corporation on its dividend income. For this reason, lower effective tax rates can be claimed if the recipient corporation demonstrates that its expenses are less than these portions. This will be the case, in particular, if the investing corporation is a pure holding company with comparatively insignificant expenses. The partial exemption of dividend income is not available to French individual residents, or French corporations whose holdings amount to less than 20 percent, or are in the form of bearer shares.

[19] Assume that a French corporation owning 50 percent or more of a Swiss corporation receives from the latter a dividend of $95.00 ($100.00 less 5 percent Swiss withholding tax) and that this dividend is collected through a French bank. The French bank is required to withhold a dividend tax of $22.80 (24 percent of $95.00). The French corporation is liable for income tax, at the rate of 50 percent, on 5 percent of the net dividend after deduction of withholding tax, or $1.80 (50 percent of 5 percent of $72.20). The total French tax on the dividend thus amounts to $24.60.

[20] Assuming that the French corporation, described in the preceding footnote, collects a dividend direct, the income tax on the distribution amounts to $2.37 (50 percent of 5 percent of $95.00). No further tax is payable if the recipient corporation retains the dividend. Assuming that it redistributes the balance of the dividend, or $92.63, to its own shareholders, it must withhold dividend tax of $22.23 (24 percent of $92.63) on the distribution. In this case, the total French tax on the dividend again amounts to $24.60, as in the preceding example.

The system of limiting the taxation of intercompany dividends to a fraction of the distribution is also followed by Belgium. Under the new Belgian Income Tax Law, a Belgian corporation is, in general, required to include 15 percent of the dividends received from another (Belgian or foreign) corporation in taxable income. The taxable portion of the dividend is limited to 5 percent in the case of manufacturing or mining corporations under certain conditions.[21] The taxable portions of 5 percent or 15 percent are computed on net dividend income—that is, they are reduced by foreign withholding taxes.

The Italian schedular tax on the movable wealth of individuals or corporations (*ricchezza mobile* tax), which was described earlier, has a territorial nature. It follows that dividend income from foreign sources, like income from direct foreign business operations, is not subject to this tax. Such income, however, is included in the base of the supplementary income taxes—the complementary tax on individuals and the corporation tax. Since dividends which an Italian corporation receives from another Italian corporation are specifically exempted from the schedular tax, intercompany dividends in effect are treated alike, regardless of the domestic or foreign origin of the income.

A different approach, followed by the Federal Republic of Germany, involves elective use of the flat rate of 25 percent for dividends as well as the other types of income described earlier. To encourage corporate investment in countries with which West Germany does not presently have a tax treaty, the German corporation or other taxable business entity is permitted to apply the 25 percent flat rate on certain dividend income from nontreaty countries. Taxation at the flat rate can be claimed by a corporate shareholder owning at least 25 percent of the capital of a foreign corporation engaged in certain activities.[22] This method, to some extent, was designed to equalize the tax treatment of dividends from nontreaty countries with that of similar income from treaty countries. Its use, as an alternative to the foreign tax credit, is optional with the taxpayer. Flat rate taxation is, in general, more advantageous to the taxpayer than the foreign tax

---

[21] The value of the investment in the stock of other corporations must not exceed 50 percent of the paid-in capital of the corporation receiving the dividend, or 50 percent of the latter's paid-in capital plus reserves and the appreciation in the value of fixed assets which is recorded on the books.

[22] These activities are the same as those described earlier which are a condition for the application of the flat tax rate for income from direct foreign business operations— that is, the foreign corporation must produce or sell property abroad, render services abroad, or import merchandise from a foreign country to Germany. These limitations are designed to preclude the application of the tax privilege to distributions by foreign holding companies.

credit if the foreign country imposes no withholding tax or imposes a tax at a lower rate than the flat rate, and it is apt to preserve the benefit of foreign tax incentives as exemptions or reduced rates.

Foreign Tax Credit

The use of foreign tax credits to relieve double taxation on foreign-source income has been described. The United Kingdom, Japan, Canada, and the Federal Republic of Germany also provide relief from double taxation of foreign-source dividends through the foreign tax credit device. For corporate residents of the United Kingdom and Japan, the foreign tax credit constitutes the only form of relief available for dividend income of this kind. Canadian corporations are entitled to exclude foreign dividends from their taxable income. In the Federal Republic of Germany, the foreign tax credit merely supplements more effective methods of preventing double taxation.

Dividends which a company in the United Kingdom receives from another U.K. company are subject to neither income tax (standard tax) nor profit tax in the hands of the recipient entity; they are fully exempt. These methods for avoiding the double taxation of corporate profits do not apply to distributions received from foreign corporations. However, persons not domiciled in the United Kingdom are taxed on foreign dividends only if this income is remitted to the United Kingdom.[23]

Under the British rules, both individuals and corporations can claim the tax credit for foreign taxes imposed on the dividend (direct credit) and for a proportionate part of the income tax paid by the foreign corporation (indirect or deemed-paid credit). In effect, the tax on the foreign dividend cannot exceed the British tax rate or the foreign rate, whichever is higher.

The foreign tax credit extended by Japan is modeled on U. S. rules. A Japanese corporation can claim both the credit for foreign withholding taxes imposed on the dividend and a deemed-paid credit, computed on the grossed-up dividend, for foreign income taxes paid if it owns at least 25 percent of the foreign corporation. Corporations can choose between the per country limitation and the overall limitation on the foreign tax credit. Under some of the tax treaties concluded by Japan, a credit for

---

[23] The remittance rule applies primarily to individual taxpayers. In an unusual case, it may apply to a corporation which, although "resident" in the United Kingdom (because it is managed and controlled there), is not "domiciled" in the United Kingdom. For British tax purposes, the domicile of a corporation is determined by its place of incorporation, *Gasque v. I. R. Com'rs.* (1940) 23 T. C. 210 (K. B.).

"spared" foreign taxes is available to resident corporations for dividend income from less developed countries.

As discussed above, the foreign tax credit extended by the Federal Republic of Germany is offered as an alternative to the taxation of dividend income from nontreaty countries at a flat rate. If, however, a tax treaty does not fully remove the double taxation of dividend income, the credit is also available in connection with dividend and certain other income from treaty countries. This applies, in particular, to foreign withholding taxes imposed by the source country.

Relief under Tax Treaties

Sweden, as noted earlier, provides no unilateral relief for dividend income from foreign sources. However, substantial relief from double taxation is provided under the numerous tax treaties concluded by Sweden. In general, this treaty relief on dividends takes one of two forms. Under some of the treaties, Sweden has agreed to extend its intercompany dividend exemption, which as a matter of statutory law applies only to domestic intercompany dividends, to distributions received by a Swedish corporation from a corporation in the other contracting country. Depending on the provisions of the individual treaty, this relief may apply regardless of the relative size of the investment;[24] or it may be limited to distributions made by a subsidiary of the Swedish corporation.[25] Alternatively, some other treaties provide for a credit of foreign tax against the Swedish tax on the dividend. In default of treaty provisions, limiting of Swedish taxation to the net dividend received (gross foreign dividend reduced by foreign withholding tax) is the only relief available.

Taxation of Interest, Rentals, Royalties, and Other Income from Capital

Among the countries included in this survey, a distinction can be made between those which offer no specific tax benefits to foreign income from capital and those which extend such benefits in the form of exemptions or reduced tax rates.

The first-named group of countries includes Canada, the Federal Republic of Germany, Japan, the Netherlands, Sweden, Switzerland, and the United Kingdom. The absence, in some of these countries, of elaborate rules defining the domestic or foreign source of income from capital is

---

[24] Treaties with Canada, France, Japan, South Africa, and the United Kingdom.
[25] Treaties with Belgium, Italy, and the Netherlands.

explained by the absence of unilateral tax relief for income of this type.[26] Sweden does not recognize any distinction in the tax treatment of domestic and foreign income from capital except by permitting its residents to report foreign income from this source after deducting foreign withholding taxes. The Netherlands taxes foreign income from capital in the same manner as domestic income with one minor exception.[27] Switzerland grants preferential tax treatment only to income from foreign real estate.[28]

Canada, Germany, Japan, and the United Kingdom grant relief through the device of the foreign tax credit. Since the application of the credit is necessarily restricted to foreign taxes on income which is considered foreign income according to the law of the taxpayer's domicile, these countries have developed relatively elaborate rules determining the source of the income.

For British tax purposes, interest, royalties, and other income from intangible property is generally considered foreign-source income if the tax residence of the payor of the income (as defined under the general rules summarized in the section on tax residence) is outside the United Kingdom. The source of income from tangible property, however, is determined by reference to the physical location of the income-producing property.

Under the Canadian rules, the source of real estate rentals and royalties for mining and petroleum rights is the income-producing property. Accordingly, it appears that such income will be considered foreign if the property is located abroad. Although the question is unsettled, there is strong support for the proposition that the source of interest income is where the debtor is resident. Presumably, the same rule applies to royalties other than mineral royalties.

Somewhat more elaborate source rules apply in the Federal Republic of Germany. For German tax purposes, interest is considered to be from foreign sources if the tax residence of the debtor is located abroad, or if the debt is secured by foreign real estate. Royalties other than mineral royalties

---

[26] However, it should be remembered that in some of the countries which apply schedular classifications of income, income from capital may be reclassified under another category if it is functionally related. For example, royalty income may be classified as business income if realized in a business, or as personal service income received by an inventor. These reclassifications may affect the applicable source rules.

[27] The exception applies to interest on a debt which is secured by foreign real estate, provided that the debt is not evidenced by a bond or other negotiable instrument, and that the interest is subject to tax in the source country.

[28] This exemption covers all income from foreign real estate, including capital gains from the sale or other disposition thereof. It is applied by reducing Swiss tax in the proportion of gross foreign income to total gross income.

and other income from intangible property or rights are treated as foreign-source income if the patent, process, or trademark is licensed for utilization abroad. The source of real estate rentals and mineral royalties is determined by the situs of the income-producing property, while rentals of tangible personal property are classified as "income from miscellaneous sources" whose characterization as domestic or foreign is determined by the tax residence of the payor of the income.

Under the Italian income tax system, different rules apply for purposes of the tax on movable wealth (*ricchezza mobile* tax) on the one hand, and the supplementary income taxes on individuals and corporations, on the other. Even within the field of the *ricchezza mobile* tax, which has territorial character, the rules vary for the different subclassifications of income that are included under that category. Interest is classified as "income from capital" and exempt from the *ricchezza mobile* tax unless derived from Italian sources as defined by law.[29] Royalties, on the other hand, are classified as commercial or industrial income and as such exempt only if they originate in a foreign permanent establishment. As in the case of business income from foreign sources, the exemptions of foreign income from capital for purposes of the *ricchezza mobile* tax do not extend to the corporation tax or, to the extent that the income is remitted to Italy, the complementary tax on individuals.

In France, the rule of territoriality does not restrict the taxation of the types of income discussed here, except income from foreign real property. As stated before, this rule is, in effect, limited to the business income of a French corporation that is realized through a foreign permanent establishment or certain business transactions consummated abroad. It follows that interest, royalties, and similar income derived from foreign sources is taxed to a French corporation unless the income originates in a foreign permanent establishment. It also follows that such income will generally be taxed to an individual resident or domiciliary of France, except an alien domiciliary under certain conditions.[30] However, all income from real property situated abroad is exempt from tax.

An elaborate system of reduced tax rates for foreign income from capital applies in Belgium. This system is complicated by the method of

[29] Interest income is deemed to be from Italian sources under one of the following conditions: (1) if paid by an Italian government agency (national, provincial, or municipal); (2) if paid by an Italian corporation or an individual resident or domiciliary of Italy; (3) if the debt is secured by real estate situated in Italy; (4) if the debt is evidenced by a public instrument (notarial deed) executed in Italy.

[30] On condition that the income is subject to a general income tax in the country of which the taxpayer is a citizen.

prepayments of Belgian tax (*precomptes mobiliers*) and statutory credits for foreign taxes (*credits d'impot*) which are applied against the assessed income tax and may eliminate it completely, as shown in the example below.

A Belgian corporation derives interest or royalty income of B. fr. 100,000 from a foreign source. It is assumed that a foreign tax of 10 percent is withheld from the income. Upon receipt of the income, the Belgian corporation makes the required prepayment of 15 percent of the net income received (B. fr. 13,500). In computing its assessed income tax, the corporation claims credit for this prepayment as well as the foreign withholding tax, the rate of which is fixed for credit purposes at 15 percent regardless of the actual foreign rate.

Gross foreign income	B. fr.	100,000
Less—foreign withholding tax of 10 percent		10,000
Net foreign income includable in tax base		90,000
Tentative corporation tax at 30 percent		27,000
Less—credits against tax:		
Prepayment	B. fr. 13,500	
Foreign withholding tax (15 percent of net income)	13,500	
		27,000
Balance of assessed income tax		None

In effect, the prepayment of 15 percent of the net income received is the final tax on the foreign income. A corresponding rule applies in the case of individual taxpayers.

Income from foreign real estate is taxed at one-half the regular rate to individual residents of Belgium, and at one-fourth of the regular rate to Belgian corporations. Depending on whether the applicable corporate tax is 30 percent or 35 percent, the effective tax rate on such income is 7.5 percent or 8.75 percent.

Taxation of Capital Gains

All ten countries extend special tax treatment to gains from the sale or other disposition of property, unless such gains are realized in the operation of a business or in the course of another taxable activity. The distinction between capital receipts on the one hand, and business profits on the other, is made in different ways. For example, in the United Kingdom and Canda, such factors as the intent of the taxpayer, the type of property disposed of, the frequency of sales, and their relationship to the taxpayer's ordinary activities are relevant; in these countries, corporations and other business entities can realize nontaxable capital gains. In the European countries, the characteristics of the person disposing of the property are given more weight. Under these systems, all transactions of a corporation or other commercial entity are considered business transactions, and all income of these entities is considered business income because of the taxpayer's form of organization. Thus, the question whether certain income qualifies as capital gain does not arise as far as commercial entities are concerned.

Within this general framework, the tax treatment of capital gains varies from country to country. Complete exemption of capital gains is the rule in Canada and, except for gain from certain short-term transactions and the disposition of domestic or foreign patents, in the United Kingdom. Sweden exempts gain from the sale of nonbusiness real estate held for more than ten years, or nonbusiness property other than real estate held for more than five years, and taxes only a fraction of the gain if the property is held for certain minimum periods below these limits (seven years for real property and two years for personal property). Under the Japanese rules, corporations can claim 50 percent of capital gains in taxable income but only for gains arising from the expropriation of property.

When capital gains are taxable under the rules of the various countries, these rules generally apply to foreign as well as domestic gains. However, there are a few significant exceptions to this rule. Under Swiss federal and cantonal tax law, gain from the disposition of real property situated abroad is exempt. For purposes of the Swedish rules on capital gain taxation, foreign real property is treated as personal property, so that gain from the disposition of such property is fully exempt if the holding period exceeds five years, and only partially taxed if it is over two but less than five years.

In countries which tax capital gains and provide relief from double taxation through the foreign tax credit, the characterization of the gain as domestic or foreign income becomes important if the country in which the property is located also imposes a capital gains tax. In general, the rule is that tangible, movable, or immovable property has its situs at the place where it is physically located at the time of the disposition. The situs of patents, trademarks, and other registered rights is usually determined by the place where the right is registered. The situs of corporate shares is usually deemed to be the place where the issuing corporation is resident according to the law of the taxpayer's domicile, while that of bonds and other debt instruments may be the domicile of the creditor or the place where the certificates are physically located at the time of disposition.

Taxation on Income Earned in
Less Developed Countries

Among the industrialized countries, the United Kingdom, the Federal Republic of Germany, Japan, and Sweden extend certain tax benefits to investments in less developed countries.[31] Existing benefits of this kind are the foreign tax credit for taxes that are forgiven, or "spared," under the rules of the less developed country and tax deferral in the resident country for investments in less developed countries.

Tax-Sparing Credit

A foreign credit for taxes that are forgiven, or "spared," by a less developed country, usually in connection with an industrial development program conducted by the latter, is included in a limited number of recent tax treaties. The tax-sparing feature is incorporated in treaties of the United Kingdom with Pakistan (1961), Malta (1962), and Israel (1963);[32] treaties of the Federal Republic of Germany with India (1959) and Israel;[33] treaties concluded by Japan with India (1960), Pakistan (1959), and Singapore (1961); and treaties of Sweden with Ireland (1959) and Israel (1959).[34]

Under the treaties of the United Kingdom, the credit can be claimed, under precisely defined conditions, for taxes that are waived by the other treaty country on new industrial investments, or for the benefit of foreign technicians and teachers. The treaties concluded by Japan, in addition, grant a credit for the taxes of the source country that are forgiven in connection with the payment of interest and (except for the treaty with Pakistan) dividends to Japanese creditors and shareholders of local corporations. Considering that Japanese investment in India and Pakistan is predominantly in the form of loans, the interest credit is significant to Japanese investors.

[31] Under the United States Revenue Act of 1962, the rules on the attribution to U. S. shareholders of certain income of controlled foreign corporations do not apply to the income of such corporations from qualifying investments in less developed countries. This tax benefit is not strictly comparable to those discussed in the text.

[32] The statutory authorization to the British government to conclude tax treaties which incorporate the tax-sparing feature is section 17 of the Finance Act of 1961, 9 & 10 Eliz. 2, Ch. 36.

[33] The tax treaty between Germany and Israel is awaiting ratification.

[34] The application of the tax-sparing principle under the Swedish treaties is extremely limited.

The tax-sparing provisions in the treaties of the Federal Republic of Germany with India and Israel are limited to taxes on interest and dividends that are waived by those countries. Since, as explained above, profits from direct foreign operations in those countries are excluded from the tax base of German residents, as long as such operations are conducted as a "permanent establishment," tax-sparing provisions in connection with branch operations are unnecessary. For the same reason, tax sparing cannot be claimed for dividends if the investment in the Indian or Israeli corporation amounts to 25 percent or more.[35] Under an unusual provision in the treaty between Germany and India, the credit for the Indian tax on interest amounts to at least 50 percent of the German tax. In effect, the treaty establishes a minimum credit which applies whenever the Indian tax, whether through tax sparing or low rates, falls below the minimum.

Tax Deferral

Under a recent (1961) amendment to the income tax laws of the Federal Republic of Germany, corporate taxpayers can obtain tax deferral for investments in less developed countries under certain conditions. This tax benefit is granted in the form of a deductible investment reserve, whose amount must be restored to taxable income over a period of five years, beginning with the third year after the year in which the investment was made. Qualifying investments can be made in the shares of corporations or the capital of unincorporated business associations created in a less developed country, or through the transfer of capital to a branch or other dependent establishment maintained in such a country. Investments in foreign holding companies, so-called tax-haven corporations, and certain foreign shipping companies do not as a rule qualify for deferral. Since foreign aid through tax deferral is a novel concept, the technical rules on forming the investment reserve are largely tentative, and it is anticipated that the requirements for forming the reserve will be liberalized.

[35] See earlier discussion of intercorporate dividends.

Index

Index

141